DAYS THAT I'LL REMEMBER

SPENDING TIME WITH

JOHN LENNON

&

YOKO ONO

DAYS THAT I'LL REMEMBER

SPENDING TIME WITH

JOHN LENNON

&

YOKO ONO

JONATHAN COTT

OMNIBUS PRESS

This edition published by arrangement with Doubleday, an imprint of The Knopf Doubleday
Publishing Group, a division of Random House, Inc.

ISBN: 978.1.78305.044.4
Order No: OP55341

Grateful acknowledgment is made to Yoko Ono for permission to reprint previously published
and unpublished material from interviews between the author and John Lennon and Yoko Ono,
portions of which originally appeared in different form in *Rolling Stone* magazine on November
23, 1968, March 18, 1971, and December 23, 2010.

Book design by Pei Loi Koay
Cover designed by Fresh Lemon.

Exclusive Distributors
Music Sales Limited,
14/15 Berners Street,
London, W1T 3LJ.

Macmillan Distribution Services,
56 Parkwest Drive
Derrimut, Vic 3030,
Australia.

Every effort has been made to trace the copyright holders of the photographs in this
book but one or two were unreachable. We would be grateful if the photographers
concerned would contact us.

Printed in the EU

A catalogue record for this book is available from the British Library.

Visit Omnibus Press on the web at www.omnibuspress.com

We were a wizard and a witch
In a moment of freedom.

—YOKO ONO, "YOU'RE THE ONE"

AUTHOR'S NOTE

In *Days That I'll Remember*, I am presenting for the first time the complete versions of all of my significant interviews and conversations with John Lennon and Yoko Ono; all of them contain new and previously unpublished material.

I first met and interviewed John in September 1968 in London; it was the first extensive interview he gave after he and Yoko had become lovers and collaborators four months earlier. A shorter version of this conversation appeared in *Rolling Stone* magazine's first anniversary issue, dated November 23, 1968.

John once told me: "Yoko is the most famous unknown artist. Everybody knows her name, but nobody knows what she does"; and in 1970, with his encouragement and participation, I wrote one of the first extensive profiles of Yoko, a shortened version of which appeared in the March 18, 1971, issue of *Rolling Stone*. The complete version of that profile appears here for the first time.

When John and Yoko moved permanently to New York City in the early 1970s, I would run into them at odd times and places, and the three of us would occasionally meet up for dinner. In this book I am including an account of one of the most unusual and lively of our dinner conversations that took place on March 17, 1971.

I saw and interviewed John on December 5, 1980, three days before his death. It was his last print interview, and most of our nine-hour conversation appeared for the first time in the December 23, 2010, issue of *Rolling Stone*. A greatly expanded, and now complete, version of that interview is included here.

On March 14, 2012, I interviewed Yoko in Stockholm, Sweden, especially for this book; this is the first publication of that interview.

In *Days That I'll Remember*, I have incorporated several brief passages from my essay "John Lennon: How He Became Who He Was," which first appeared in an anthology I co-edited entitled *The Ballad of John and Yoko*, published by Doubleday in 1982; as well as from my essay "Children of Paradise: Back to Where We Once Belonged," which appeared in *Rolling Stone*'s tenth anniversary issue in 1977.

DAYS THAT I'LL REMEMBER

SPENDING TIME WITH

JOHN LENNON

&

YOKO ONO

INTRODUCTION

"Is there anybody going to listen to my story / All about the girl who came to stay?" John Lennon asked in his song "Girl" on the Beatles' 1965 *Rubber Soul* album. Three years later, on the afternoon of September 17, 1968, I found myself ringing the doorbell of a basement flat at 34 Montagu Square in London. After a few seconds, an effervescent twenty-seven-year-old man with shoulder-length dark-brown hair—dressed in a black sweater, jeans, and white tennis shoes and wearing round, wire-rimmed granny glasses—opened the door. "Come in, come in!" he said, then led me into the living room where he introduced me to the extraordinary girl who had come to stay, invited me to sit down on a couch, and asked me if I would like to listen to his story.

Days That I'll Remember is my own personal story about the times that I spent with John Lennon and Yoko Ono

1

over a period of forty-five years. It is a story that began on a cold New York City morning in December 1963 during the first semester of my senior year at Columbia College. My clock radio had woken me up at 7:30. Craving another few minutes of sleep—even if it meant that I would arrive late for my much-dreaded class in set theory—I decided to turn the radio off, but just as my hand was reaching for the knob, I suddenly heard a male voice shouting out "*One-Two-Three-FAW!*" And then: "She was just seventeen / If you know what I mean!" Just as it happens in the song, my heart went *BOOM*, and I immediately knew that, from that moment on, "I Saw Her Standing There" would be the wake-up call for my entire life.

"*I* can't wake you up," John Lennon once said. "*You* can wake you up." But, luckily, the Beatles were going to remind me to do so—"Woke up, fell out of bed / Dragged a comb across my head." Sometimes, however, it seemed as if the Beatles themselves were a dream from which you really never wanted to awake. In fact, many people came to think of the four Beatles as symbolic dream figures and presences—like the four evangelists, the four seasons, the four phases of the moon, the four corners of the earth—and in an elementary sense, each Beatle, in the way he became defined by his face, gestures, voice, and songs, took on an archetypal role: Paul, sweet and sensitive; John, restless and rebellious; George, mysterious and mystical; Ringo, childlike but commonsensical.

"None of us would've made it alone," John once explained, "because Paul wasn't strong enough, I didn't have enough girl-appeal, George was too quiet, and Ringo was the drummer. But we thought everyone would be able to dig at least one of us, and that's how it turned out." For me, John Lennon was always the One. He had attained instant hero status in my eyes from the moment I first heard about the Beatles' 1963 Royal Command Performance at London's Prince of Wales Theatre with the Queen Mother and Princess Margaret in attendance. Introducing the song "Twist and Shout," John stepped up to the microphone and announced: "For our last number, I'd like to ask your help. The people in the cheap seats, clap your hands. And the rest of you, if you'd just rattle your jewelry."

A century and a half earlier, in 1812, another one of my heroes, Ludwig van Beethoven, was walking down the street of a Bavarian resort town with the distinguished German writer Johann Wolfgang von Goethe when they happened to cross paths with Empress Maria Ludovica and a retinue of nobles. Goethe stepped aside, doffed his hat, and kowtowed deeply. Beethoven, who rolled over for no one, strode right through their midst and admonished the obsequious writer, reminding him that nobles were a dime a dozen "but there are only two of *us!*" As the Beatles, in a similar vein, once observed: "Her Majesty's a pretty nice girl / But she doesn't have a lot to say." (Ironically, as I would later discover, Yoko Ono herself could claim a lineage purporting to go back to a ninth-century Japanese emperor, and in this book I discuss what is probably for most people her unfamiliar family history.)

As John developed as a person and an artist throughout the twelve years that I knew him, he continually revealed ever-increasing facets of himself both to me and to his millions of admirers, even inviting us to accompany him on his journey down to Strawberry Fields to observe him unpeeling the layers of his identity, as well as delving into and exploring his own mind, which was, in fact, Strawberry Fields itself. Alluding to the well-known image of the giraffe going by a window, John once said, "People are always just seeing little bits of it, but I try and see the whole . . . not just in my life, but the whole universe, the whole game." He was both Nowhere Man and Eggman, he contained multitudes, and of these, one and all, he wove the song of himself.

It was an all-embracing song that included anthems ("Give Peace a Chance") and dream collages ("Revolution 9"), meditations ("Strawberry Fields Forever") and calls to action ("Power to the People"), comic portraits ("Polythene Pam") and cosmic statements ("Across the Universe"). And it was a song that expressed an astonishing range of contrasting states of feelings and emotions: weariness ("I'm So Tired") and wakefulness ("Instant Karma!"), need ("Help!") and independence ("Good Morning Good Morning"), depression ("You've Got to Hide Your Love Away") and elation ("Whatever Gets You Thru the Night"), and pleasure ("I Feel Fine") and pain ("Yer Blues").

4

Never afraid to expose and explore his own vulnerabilities, John audaciously confronted the reality of his own irrepressible jealousy—as he once amusingly said, "I get jealous of the mirror"—and dealt with this self-feeding demon in Beatles songs like "No Reply," "You Can't Do That," and "Run for Your Life," lifting its line "I'd rather see you dead, little girl, / Than to be with another man," from Elvis Presley's "Baby, Let's Play House." But it was in one of his most remarkable songs, "Jealous Guy," that he entered daringly into jealousy's realm, describing with astonishing exactitude the manner by which it manifests itself in our bodies—heart beating fast, shivering inside, swallowing one's pain—and in so doing, allowed it to be experienced as something rich and strange.

Most remarkably, and unlike almost any other male rock songwriter I can think of, John sang about his mother. As he once remarked: "I used to feel I wouldn't be singing 'She Loves You' at thirty, but I didn't know I would be singing about my mother!" And he did so in two extraordinary songs. In "Julia," he says goodbye to her—picturing her as a "morning moon"—and tells her that he has been swept away by an "ocean child" with "seashell eyes" and "hair of floating sky" that shimmers in the sun. (The name Yoko means "ocean child" in Japanese.) And in his song "Mother," which he wrote just two years later, he says goodbye to Julia for the second and last time, screaming out and thereby exorcising the inexorable pain he had for so long harbored within himself because of what he felt was her rejection of him when

he was six years old. Ironically, the first line of that song—
"Mother, you had me / but I never had you"—echoes to a T
the jocularly self-deflating opening of "Norwegian Wood":
"I once had a girl, / or should I say, she once had me."

The art and life of a person who contains multitudes is
usually filled with contradictions. John Lennon was a born
leader. It was he who brought Paul into the Quarrymen
(Paul brought George, and George, Ringo), and it was he
who, early on, had a sense of being out of the ordinary ("I
was hip in kindergarten . . . When I was about twelve I used
to think: I must be a genius, but nobody's noticed"). But he
was a leader who unstintingly shared his creative powers in
collaboration with Paul McCartney and Yoko Ono.

He was an unreconstructable rock 'n' roller whose life
was forever changed by "Heartbreak Hotel" ("When I heard
it, I dropped everything") and "Long Tall Sally" ("When I
heard it, it was so great I couldn't speak"), and who once
thought—before he met the girl who came to stay—that
"avant-garde" was French for "bullshit." Yet he was always
experimenting with tapes played backward, tape loops,
and sound montages, and in "Revolution 9," he created an
avant-garde masterpiece.

He was sometimes insecure and sometimes boastful ("Part
of me suspects that I'm a loser and the other part thinks I'm
God almighty"). He was a trusting and believing person
who frequently—and, as it turned out, presciently—spoke
of his own sense of mistrust and paranoia ("Paranoia," he

once said, "is just a heightened sense of awareness"). If he occasionally seemed stubborn, he at the same time developed a high degree of flexibility that enabled him to move on, to take risks—personally and artistically—and to live continually in the present ("Some people like Ping-Pong, other people like digging over graves. . . . Some people will do anything rather than be here now . . . *I don't believe in yesterday*"). And finally, he was a leader who renounced his crown and empire in order to be true to himself ("It's pretty hard when you are Caesar and everyone is saying how wonderful you are and they're giving you all the goodies and the girls, it's pretty hard to break out of that, to say, 'Well, I don't want to be king, I want to be real' "). It was, of course, the girl who came to stay who would become his life-teacher and soul guide. As he informed us in his song "One Day (at a Time)," he was the fish and she was the sea, he was the apple and she was the tree, he was the door and she was the key. Simply, Yoko enabled John to become who he was.

"Two minds, one destiny" was the way John once characterized his and Yoko's relationship. Together, they attempted to re-create paradise on earth—"Just a boy and a little girl, / Trying to change the whole wide world," as John described Yoko and himself in his song "Isolation"—and offered to take everyone along with them for the ride. Many people—querulous cynics as well as crestfallen Beatles fans who wanted John only on his own and only for themselves—sneered at the thought and refused to accept the ticket.

But trying to change the world by taking one's clothes off, greeting journalists in bed, and sending acorns to world leaders—with an accompanying letter requesting that they plant the acorns in their gardens and "grow two oak trees for world peace"—wasn't exactly the most persuasive of images for conveying the notion of two great romantic lovers. One can hardly imagine a besotted Tristan serenading his beloved with a song called "Oh Isolde" and then, as John did in his song "Oh Yoko," deliriously calling out her name "in the middle of a cloud," "in the middle of the bath," and "in the middle of a shave." But it was exactly John and Yoko's endearingly naïve and ludic way of being in the world that made them so real and believable a modern romantic couple—only two fools could be so much in love!

Both of them joyfully embraced their roles as Holy Fools—as the Bible says, "God hath chosen the foolish things of the world to confound the wise"—and, in their own tongue-in-cheek way, John and Yoko lived lives that acted out in the everyday world the archetypal dramas of the imagination. I have always thought of them whenever I read the heartbreaking letters of Abelard and Héloïse, the ill-starred twelfth-century French lovers—he a famous and charismatic philosopher, theologian, poet, and musician; she, his pupil, paramour, wife, and then, after their enforced parting, an abbess of a convent. As she wrote to Abelard:

You had besides, I admit, two special gifts whereby
to win at once the heart of any woman—your gifts
for composing verse and song, in which we know
other philosophers have rarely been successful. . . . The
beauty of the airs ensured that even the unlettered did
not forget you; more than anything, this made women
sigh for love of you. And as most of these songs told
of our love, they soon made me widely known and
roused the envy of many women against me. For your
manhood was adorned by every grace of mind and
body, and among the women who envied me then,
could there be one now who does not feel compelled
by my misfortune to sympathize with my loss of such
joys? Who is there who was once my enemy, whether
man or woman, who is not moved now by the compassion which is my due?

It is a letter that Yoko might have written after John's death.

Yoko still has her uncomprehending and abusive detractors, but those of her admirers who have followed her more
than fifty-year career know that what is rightfully due to her
is not only the offering of compassion to a grieving widow but
also the recognition of her extraordinary accomplishments
as a painter, sculptor, photographer, filmmaker, poet, video
artist, composer, singer-songwriter, pioneer of conceptual
and performance art, and peace activist. She is also the only
person who can be said to have worked with musicians as

radically diverse as John Cage, Ornette Coleman, and Lady Gaga; to have had nine number-one hits on the *Billboard* Dance/Club Play Chart; to have read an ode to peace at the opening ceremony for the 2006 Winter Olympic Games in Turin; and, just as the emperor Shah Jahan built the Taj Mahal in remembrance of his third wife, to have memorialized her late husband by envisioning and single-handedly creating on Videy Island in Iceland the IMAGINE PEACE TOWER—a kind of sacred flame that on a clear night can reach an altitude of about two-and-a-half miles. This tower of light is projected from a monument made of white glass tiles on which the words IMAGINE PEACE are carved in twenty-four languages. More than 1.5 million written wishes for peace have been collected by Yoko from people all over the world and will be incorporated into the tower at a future date. As the guardian of the flame throughout the more than thirty years since John's passing, Yoko has been devotedly and unwaveringly keeping his fearless and imagining spirit alive.

On the evening of December 8, 1980, I had gone to sleep around ten thirty. Just after midnight, I was woken up by the phone ringing, and I got out of bed and picked up the receiver. I heard my friend on the other end of the line crying. "Oh my god, what's wrong?" I said. "Have you heard the news?" she asked me. "What news?" I said. "I've been sleeping." And she told me that John Lennon was dead.

Rolling Stone magazine had been preparing a cover story on John and Yoko for its first issue of 1981 to mark the release of their new album, *Double Fantasy,* and the interview I had done with John on December 5 was slated to appear in that issue; it would now be devoted to his memory. Jann Wenner—the co-founder, editor, and publisher of *Rolling Stone* (and a longtime friend), who in 1967 had designated me as the magazine's first European editor—asked me if I could write up an account of what had turned out to be the last interview I would ever do with John. With a sense of emotional numbness, I hastily listened to the tapes, garnering from them as best I could a small portion of what I felt were some of the highlights of our conversation, and included them in my five-thousand-word tribute article.

Yoko Ono had requested that on Sunday, December 14, at 2:00 p.m. eastern standard time, people around the world who wished to do so should engage in a ten-minute silent vigil in memory of John. In the United States, some eight thousand radio stations ceased broadcasting for ten minutes. Thirty thousand people gathered in Liverpool; and I, along with several of my friends, joined more than 250,000 people in Central Park to honor John. At precisely two o'clock, the only sounds to be heard were the whirring blades of the helicopters flying overhead; they reminded me of the

Indian-inspired tamboura drone played by George Harrison on the recording of John's "Tomorrow Never Knows" ("Turn off your mind, relax and float downstream / It is not dying, it is not dying"). John had told the Beatles producer George Martin that on that song he wanted to sound like "the Dalai Lama chanting from a mountaintop, miles away."

I had never transcribed my last interview with John. I had written my tribute article and felt that I was going to be too upset to listen to John's voice on my tapes anytime soon, so I stowed them away in the recesses of my closet. At the beginning of 2010, however, it dawned on me that John would have turned seventy on October 9 and, furthermore, that December 8 would mark the thirtieth anniversary of his death. I actually hadn't thought about those tapes since 1980, but I now decided that after so many years, I should attempt to find them. Long-neglected, they were by now certainly moldering and perhaps even degrading. So I went rummaging through the clutter of my closet, and after half an hour I found the tapes, bound together by two mopey-looking rubber bands. A week later, I put on my headphones and began the laborious process of transcribing the tapes from beginning to end in longhand on three legal-size notepads. On those magical strips of magnetic tape, I once again heard the joyous, vibrant, subversive, acerbic, fearless, outrageously funny, human-hearted words of a man whose lips had undoubtedly kissed, at least in his dreams, the gab-inducing Blarney Stone.

It took me ten inspired but wearying days to complete the transcribing, and upon falling asleep after accomplishing my task, I had a dream that I will always remember but one that I never recounted to anyone, anticipating that some people would imagine that I had calculatedly and spuriously constructed a self-dramatizing personal myth. But the dream was real. In it, John and I were sitting on a rug on the floor of an apartment—much as he and I had actually done when I first interviewed him in 1968 in his Montagu Square flat in London—facing each other like two ancient shamanic bards and drinking mint tea. I had set up my tape recorder to begin my interview . . . but suddenly, and sickeningly, I realized that John wasn't aware that he was dead, and that I must, at all costs, be careful not to let him know that he was and be certain not to ask him about his and Yoko's future plans. John began the conversation by speaking the same words that he had used when I interviewed him for the last time in his Dakota apartment: "You don't have to rush, we've got hours and hours and hours." And at that moment in my dream, I recalled the first two lines of John's song "Working Class Hero," which I had always felt were among the most piercing and heartbreaking words he ever wrote: "As soon as you're born they make you feel small / By giving you no time instead of it all."

Somehow, I managed to carry on with the interview until, as it was coming to its end, John said to me, "What song would you like to hear me sing right now? Just the first one that comes to mind." So I said, "I think I'd like to hear 'Instant Karma!' " and he began to sing it to me. And when he got to the words "Why in the world are we here? / Surely not to live in pain and fear," he looked hard at me to make sure I would *really* hear them. It was at that moment that I woke up—astonished, sad, happy, upset, but grateful to have been present at such an encounter—and thought to myself: "Wow! I saw John Lennon last night, and he is as alive as you or me!"

W elcome to the inner sanctum!" said John Lennon, as he greeted me with high-spirited, mock ceremoniousness at the entrance to Yoko Ono's office in their ground-floor apartment in the Dakota—the quasi-Gothic, castle-like edifice with its gables, gargoyles, and wrought-iron gates on New York City's Upper West Side. I removed my shoes and entered an iridescent, high-ceilinged, white-carpeted room, and Yoko, who was seated at a large gold-inlaid desk, got up to say hello.

It was Friday, December 5, 1980. *Rolling Stone* was preparing a cover story on John and Yoko for its first issue of 1981, and I had come to interview John on the occasion of the release of his and Yoko's new album, *Double Fantasy*. It had been a long while since they had talked to the press. With the birth of their son, Sean, in 1975, John and Yoko had undertaken what they called "the Spring Cleaning of our minds" and had ceased stoking what Joni Mitchell once referred to as the "star maker machinery." For five years, they made no records, created no new music or artworks, and made no public appearances. And while Yoko looked after the family business, John became a self-styled househusband who spent his time taking care of his son and engaging in domestic chores. One thinks of the Greek historian Herodotus's description of some of the remarkable customs practiced by the Egyptians in the fifth-century B.C.: "Women attend market and are employed in trade, while men stay at home and do the weaving." The Lenonos—to use the name of John and Yoko's music-publishing company—seem to have run an ancient Egyptian household! Or a topsy-turvy nursery-rhyme one, where, as John informed us in his song "Cleanup Time," the queen is in the counting house "counting out the money," while the king stays in the kitchen "making bread and honey."

In an interview with journalist Chet Flippo, the media consultant Elliot Mintz—who had developed a close friendship with John and Yoko in 1971—spoke of a night when John phoned him in Los Angeles. "It was very late," Mintz recalled, "and John said, 'An incredible thing happened to me today, Elliot,' and he said it with such reverence that I thought he was going to divulge a really significant spiritual experience. So I propped myself up and said, 'Yes?' And John said, 'I baked my first loaf of bread and you can't believe how perfectly it rose, and I've taken a Polaroid photo of it and I think I can get it out to you by messenger tonight.' "

Mintz explained that John and Yoko would use a courier service instead of the mail because people would pocket their letters or packages as souvenirs when they saw either one of their names on them. "So someone would pick up the communication," Mintz elaborated, "and get on an airplane and fly with the communication wherever it was going, and then hand the communication to the person it was going to." Mintz received the Polaroid. A week or two later, he flew to New York and stopped by the Dakota. "We were sitting around the kitchen one night," Mintz said, "and John brought out an object enclosed in silver foil. It was a piece of the bread that he had saved me from his first loaf. And we broke bread together."

John had stepped outside the inner sanctum for a few minutes, and I sat down next to Yoko on an enormous pearl-white plush couch. In this gently lit, immaculate office, I noticed a black upright piano and, on a wall above it, a painted portrait showing John and Sean, both with shoulder-length hair, sitting on a beach in Bermuda; an ivory-and-jade inlaid oak box resting on a coffee table; and several glass vitrines containing ancient Egyptian artifacts, which Yoko valued for their beauty and magical properties.

Then I looked up, and, as if I were rising—rather than

falling—into a dream, I suddenly realized that the entire ceiling was in fact a supernal trompe l'oeil sky filled with floating and drifting gossamer clouds. *"Above us only sky."* And I was immediately reminded of the open letter written by John and Yoko and published on the back page of *The New York Times* on May 27, 1979. Entitled "A Love Letter from John and Yoko to People Who Ask Us What, When, and Why," it had concluded: "Remember, our silence is a silence of love and not of indifference. Remember, we are writing in the sky instead of on paper—that's our song. Lift your eyes and look up in the sky . . . and you will see that you are walking in the sky, which extends to the ground. We are all part of the sky, more than of the ground." And although my head was still in the clouds, ensorcelled by cerulean light, I slowly brought myself back down to earth as Yoko began explaining to me how the album *Double Fantasy* came to be.

The previous spring, she recounted, John had, with her blessing, chartered the *Megan Jaye*, a forty-three-foot sloop based in Newport, Rhode Island, and set sail on June 4 with a four-member crew for the 635-mile trip to Bermuda. He had previously learned to sail on Long Island Sound where he and Yoko had a second home in Cold Spring Harbor, and for a long time had harbored a desire to undertake a long sea voyage. He would be turning forty on October 9, and, as he wrote in "Borrowed Time"—a song that he composed after the completion of his trip—"Now I am older / The future is brighter and now is the hour."

The plan was for Sean to fly with a nanny to Bermuda after John had arrived there, and father and son would then spend a three-week vacation together, swimming and sailing, while Yoko stayed at home "sorting out business," as she put it. But midway into John's navigational journey through the Bermuda Triangle, a storm broke out with gale-force winds and twenty-foot-high waves. The captain and crew fell ill, and John, not prone to seasickness, had to take over as helmsman for six hours. Buffeted by the winds and pummeled by water, he later described himself as having felt like a Viking "screaming sea chanteys and shouting at the gods." Reflecting on his adventure, John would later remark to me: "You get in a fucking boat in a 110-mile-per-hour gale and you really find out what's real or not."

He rented a stucco villa in the idyllically named Fairylands on the outskirts of Hamilton, and every day he and Sean would go swimming and build sand castles on the beach. It was here that they ran into a woman artist who mustered the courage to approach them to ask if she could paint John and Sean together. Surprisingly, John agreed. For several days, he and Sean went to her studio to pose for the portrait. When John returned to New York, he presented it to Yoko as a surprise gift, and it was this painting that I had noticed hanging on the wall above the piano in Yoko's office.

One day, John took Sean to the Bermuda Botanical Gardens where, under a cedar tree, he came across some delicate white-and-yellow flowers called a Double Fantasy. "It's a type of freesia," John explained, "but what it means to us is that if two people picture the same image at the same time, that is the secret." And then one night he wandered into Hamilton and, curious to find out what kind of music people were listening to, he went club-hopping—something he hadn't done since the mid-1970s in Los Angeles—and ended up at a spot called Disco 40. "Upstairs, they were playing disco," John would later tell me, "but downstairs I suddenly heard 'Rock Lobster' by the B-52s for the first time. Do you know it? It sounds just like Yoko's music, so I said to meself, 'It's time to get out the old ax and wake the wife up!'"

John began writing songs at a rapid pace. "Woman" apparently took him about fifteen minutes, and in one of his new songs, "Dear Yoko," he referred to his harrowing sea voyage, telling her that even in the midst of the tempest, her spirit had been watching over him. Simultaneously, Yoko, in New York, had also started writing songs. As if to confirm her idea that, as she once remarked, "you can assemble a painting with a person in the North Pole over a phone, like playing chess," she and John began to speak on the phone every day and sang each other what they had composed in between calls. During one of their conversations, John sang her "Beautiful Boy," and Yoko said, "I wrote a song, too, it's called 'Beautiful Boys.' Let me sing it to *you*." And when John came back to New York, Yoko asked him, "Do you want to do it?," and John answered "Yes."

. . .

John had now returned to the inner sanctum, and Yoko said that she'd be leaving us for a while so that we could chat. As John sat down on the couch, I told him that Yoko had informed me how *Double Fantasy* had come about, and observed that this was probably the first album ever created over the telephone. "Yeh," John said, laughing, "and it's a play. It's a *heart* play, with the emphasis on *ear* in the middle of that word!"

"I've heard that you've had a guitar hanging on the wall behind your bed for the past five or six years," I said to him, "and that you only recently took it down to play on *Double Fantasy*. Is that true?"

"I bought this beautiful electric guitar round about the period I got back with Yoko and had the baby," he replied. "It's not a normal guitar, it doesn't have a body, it's just an arm and this tubelike, toboggan-looking thing, and you can lengthen the top for the balance of it if you're sitting or standing up. I played it a little, and then just hung it up behind the bed, but I'd look at it every now and then, because it had never done a professional thing, it had never really been played. I didn't want to hide it the way one would hide an instrument because it was too painful to look at—like Artie Shaw went through a big thing and never played his clarinet again. But I used to look at it and think, 'Will I ever pull it down?'

"On top of the guitar I'd placed a wooden number nine

that some kid had sent me and a dagger Yoko had given me—a dagger made out of a bread knife from the American Civil War to cut away the bad vibes, to cut away the past symbolically. It was just like a picture that hangs there but you never really see, and then recently I realized, 'Oh, goody! I can finally find out what this guitar is all about,' and I took it down and used it in making *Double Fantasy.*"

"So that guitar wasn't gently weeping behind you for five years?" I asked.

"Mine *never* weeped," he replied. "Mine screams or it's not on at all!"

"I've been playing *Double Fantasy* a lot," I started to say to John overexcitedly, "and it's fantastic, but I've only heard it for the past three or four days and I wish I had it before—"

"How are you?" John interrupted, and looked at me with a time- and interview-stopping smile. "You don't have to rush, we've got hours and hours and hours. It's been like a reunion for us these last few weeks. The record's already up there, it's already passed the test of whatever it's supposed to pass, the public have accepted it and bought it. I'm glad, Yoko's glad, we're glad to work together again and talk to the press."

"You haven't minded answering all the usual questions?" I asked him.

"It's a game," he said, "but the whole of life is a game, isn't it? But is the implication then that the game is immoral? I mean, are we supposed to be *very* serious or just a *little* serious about it? But it *is* a very serious concern—a lot of money is put into an album, a lot of sweat and blood . . . and then having to put up with the garbage again, right? So we're doing it because we *want* to do it, and we think we can have fun with it, and people want a record, obviously, because otherwise they wouldn't have bought it.

"We recently did a very nice interview with a very nice reporter—I really enjoyed him, and he was an intelligent guy, and I don't want to hurt him in any way. But when he described me in his article, I realized he hadn't seen me at all."

"In what sense?" I asked.

"He described me as wearing wire-rimmed glasses. Now, I haven't worn wire-rimmed glasses since 1973. You see the glasses I'm wearing? They're normal, plastic, blue-frame glasses."

"Just so that I don't fall into the same trap," I said to him, "maybe you could describe to the magazine's readers what you're wearing right now."

"O.K.," John began. "Tell them that he's wearing needle-cord pants, and the same black cowboy boots he'd had made in Nudie's in 1973—"

"What's Nudie's?" I asked him.

"It's the famous cowboy shop in Hollywood where Elvis got his gold lamé suit. It's the place with the bull horns on the front, and everybody knows it."

"Except me."

"Now you do . . . And he's wearing a Calvin Klein sweater

and a torn Mick Jagger T-shirt that he got when the Stones toured in 1970 or so. I think that it belonged to a roadie and someone gave it to me. And around his neck is a small, three-part diamond heart necklace that he bought as a makeup present after an argument with Yoko many years ago and that she later gave back to him in a kind of ritual. Will that do?"

"Thanks! You've saved me."

"Anyway, it's been fun talking to people, and it's fun having your picture taken . . . well, not so much having it taken, but it's fun to see them, and in ten years you still have them. We've seen Ethan Russell, who took photos of us in 1969, and Annie Leibovitz was here. She took my first *Rolling Stone* cover photo, and she's doing her life. It's been fun seeing everyone we used to know and doing it all again—we've all survived. When did *we* first meet?"

"I met you and Yoko in London on September 17, 1968," I told him, remembering the precise date of the first of many encounters.

was just a lucky guy, at the right places at the right time. I had graduated the previous year with an M.A. in literature from the University of California at Berkeley; but the allure of academic life was fading in the light of what seemed to be the arising of a great new American social, cultural, and political awakening. For me, as for many others, the San Francisco Bay Area during the 1960s was a time when people experienced a true dramatization of life, and wherever you went "There was music in the cafés at night / and revolution in the air," as Bob Dylan sang in "Tangled Up in Blue." Two of the slogans from the May 1968 student protests in France were "Live Without Dead Time" and "Boredom Is Always Counterrevolutionary"; and on Berkeley's Telegraph Avenue and in San Francisco's Haight-Ashbury, time was alive and boredom didn't exist.

Everyone was a genius until proven otherwise. No one could know for certain when, where, and from whom the magic might suddenly manifest itself. Anyone from England or India was possibly a bearer of bliss. But so were local rock groups like the Grateful Dead, Jefferson Airplane, and Creedence Clearwater Revival; and if even a media-concocted group like the Monkees, whom John Lennon once described as "the greatest comic talents since the Marx Brothers," could bring forth the incandescent "I'm a Believer," there was no telling when a new avatar of Orpheus or David might appear.

Everyone, moreover, was given the benefit of the doubt: "Got to be good looking 'cause he's so hard to see," was the way John Lennon put it in his song "Come Together." All you needed was love; and in the Beatles' anthem of the same name, one came to realize that everything could be done and sung because everything had *already* been done and sung

27

("There's nothing you can know that isn't known / Nothing you can see that isn't shown"). It was easy: all that was needed to understand and to create was simply to recall and reconnect yourself to what had always been there in the first place.

I myself will always recall one particular January morning in Berkeley in 1966. The Beatles' album *Rubber Soul* had just been released, and as I walked down Benvenue Avenue and heard to my amazement the intermingling and overlapping sounds of "Girl," "The Word," and "Norwegian Wood" drifting out of one open window after another, it seemed to me as if the Beatles had actually realized the French poet Arthur Rimbaud's dream of creating a universal language and of transforming the world by means of a kind of acoustic alchemy, and that we were all simply following—in Rimbaud's words—"their seeings, their breathings, their bodies, their days." But across the Pacific Ocean a war was raging, so I inevitably realized that the time had come for me to awaken, at least for a while, from that dream.

I directly trace my tenaciously held pacifist beliefs and values to one of my most beloved childhood books, *The Story of Ferdinand* by Munro Leaf. Published in 1936, it tells the story of a Spanish bull whose sole desire is to sit quietly under a cork tree and smell the flowers. But one day, while Ferdinand is stretching out on the cool grass, he accidentally sits on a bumblebee. Stung, snorting, and pawing the ground in a fit of rage, he is spotted by some traveling scouts who are combing the countryside in search of the meanest and most ferocious animals, and, overjoyed by this serendipitous windfall, they straightaway cart the fiery beast off to the Plaza de Toros in Madrid. The sight of the dreaded Ferdinand the Fierce strikes fear into the hearts of the picadors, banderilleros, and matador; but when Ferdinand ambles out to the middle of the ring and espies the ravishing flowers in all the lovely ladies' hair, he is so enthralled by the fragrant odors wafting toward him that he simply sits down and refuses to budge. The outraged matador gives the pusillanimous Ferdinand a dishonorable discharge and orders that he be sent back home. "And for all I know," the author says, "he is sitting there still, under his favorite cork tree, just quietly smelling the flowers. And he is happy."

It is heartening to learn that *The Story of Ferdinand* has been translated into sixty languages and remains one of the best-selling children's books of all time, and one that might have ideally served as a bible for those tens of thousands of people who gathered in San Francisco for the Summer of Love in 1967—a moment that bore witness to John Lennon's declaration in "I Am the Walrus" that "I am he as you are he as you are me and we are all together." If Ferdinand had fortuitously wandered into the Human Be-In—the Gathering of the Tribes that took place in Golden Gate Park earlier that year and at which Timothy Leary, supposedly for the first time, uttered the phrase "Turn on, tune in, drop out"—he might have been wearing flowers on his horns and joined everyone in singing "All You Need Is Love." It is for sure that the John Lennon who sang the inspired line "Don't need a sword to cut through flowers" in "Whatever Gets You Thru the Night" would not have felt called upon to thrust in the blade but would rather have welcomed Ferdinand into the human fold with open arms.

"I come from the macho school of pretense," John had told me when I spoke with him in Yoko's office. "I was never really a street kid or a tough guy. I used to dress like a Teddy boy and identify with Marlon Brando and Elvis Presley, but I was never really in any street fights or real down-home gangs. I was just a suburban kid, imitating the rockers. But it was a big part of one's life to look tough. I spent the whole of my childhood with shoulders up around the top of me head and me glasses off because glasses were sissy, and walking in complete fear, but with the toughest-looking little face you've ever seen. I'd get into trouble just because of the way I looked. I wanted to be this tough James Dean all the time. It took a lot of wrestling to stop doing that, even though I still fall into it when I get insecure and nervous. I still drop into that I'm-a-street-kid stance, but I have to keep remembering that I never really was one. I don't know whether I would have survived on the streets of New York when I was sixteen—I was a little fruit when I see some of the kids around here. We all have to deal with that.

"That's what Yoko has taught me. I couldn't have done it alone—it had to be a female to teach me. That's it. Yoko has been telling me all the time, 'It's all right, it's all right.' I look at early pictures of meself, and I was torn between being Marlon Brando and being the sensitive poet—the Oscar Wilde part of me with the velvet, feminine side. I was always torn between the two, mainly opting for the macho side, because if you showed the other side, you were dead."

Like Ferdinand, I had no interest in ennobling and embracing the idea of "death in the afternoon," awaiting a gold-braided matador in black-velvet britches to administer the inexorable coup de grâce. In my case, the *momento de la verdad* would most likely have occurred not in a Plaza de Toros but rather in some napalmed Vietnamese hamlet. So, in spite of my misgivings about academia, I was relieved when I was informed that I had been recommended for and awarded a fellowship to study contemporary British poetry at a university in England in the fall of 1967.

While living in Berkeley, I had made friends with Ralph J. Gleason, the music columnist for the *San Francisco Chronicle*, who was responsible for having an essay I had written about the Beatles' *A Hard Day's Night* published in the San Francisco–based magazine *Ramparts*. I also got to know fellow Berkeley student Jann Wenner, who had become the entertainment editor of *Sunday Ramparts*, the magazine's spin-off newspaper, for which I wrote film and music reviews. Early in 1967, with an initial investment of $7,500, Ralph and Jann—along with Jann's future wife Jane Schindelheim—founded a semi-monthly magazine called

Rolling Stone whose goal was to document the vibrant and radical new world of rock 'n' roll, politics, and popular culture. And when I informed Jann that I would be attending a university in England that fall, he asked me if I would consider moonlighting as *Rolling Stone*'s first European editor, for which I would be paid twenty-five dollars per article, fifty dollars per interview.

Little did I know that this opportunity would prove to be a godsend, because several months before my departure overseas, I decided that it would be a good idea to begin reading in earnest some of the poetry that I was expected to be studying at the university. This turned out to be a dispiriting experience, for, with a few exceptions, I found the overwhelming majority of those poems, written by a nebulously defined, catchall group of British writers known as The Movement, to be, in the words of the British critic A. Alvarez, "glumly unadventurous." As described by him, the ideal Movement poem was "like a well-made essay; it had a beginning, a middle, and an end, and it made a point. It was carefully rhymed, rhythmically inert, and profoundly complacent." According to the poet and historian Robert Conquest, who edited the 1956 and 1963 *New Lines* anthologies in which many of the group's poems appeared, the connections among these Movement poets were "little more than a negative determination to avoid bad principles."

Emily Dickinson famously declared: "If I read a book and it makes my whole body so cold no fire ever can warm me,

I know *that* is poetry. If I feel physically as if the top of my head were taken off, I know *that* is poetry. These are the only ways I know it. Is there any other way?" Not every poem, of course, can or is intended to combust with the kinetic energy of Dickinson's "My Life had stood—a Loaded Gun," but whenever any literary tradition begins to exhibit symptoms of "the fossil or mummy character" that Ralph Waldo Emerson associated with conventional, warmed-over, and imitative writing, a countervailing force has always arisen to provide "a Spring Cleaning of the mind." Emerson himself frequently detected the renewal of the poetic impulse in the language and "uncorrupted slang" of the street. "Cut these words," he declared, "and they would bleed; they are vascular and alive; they walk and run." And in his song "Stuck Inside of Mobile with the Memphis Blues Again," Bob Dylan concurred: "Well, Shakespeare, he's in the alley / With his pointed shoes and his bells."

While I was stuck inside of The Movement, outside there were joyous poems being written and sung in alleyways, folk clubs, and coffeehouses by young students, musicians, and songwriters, much as they had done seven centuries before in the taverns, wine cellars, and bierstubes of medieval Europe. Plus ça change—although the themes of "wine, women, and song," celebrated in the famous collection of Medieval Latin songs known as the *Carmina Burana*, had now been analogously updated to "sex, drugs, and rock 'n' roll." And as abhorrent and boorish as it might have sounded to my twentieth-century English literature professors, it was patently obvious to me that the lyrics to 1960s rock songs such as John Lennon's "Strawberry Fields Forever," Van Morrison's "Madame George," Bob Dylan's "Visions of Johanna," Ray Davies's "Waterloo Sunset," John Fogerty's "Green River," Richard Manuel and Robbie Robertson's "Whispering Pines," and Mick Jagger and Keith Richards's "Have You Seen Your Mother, Baby, Standing in the Shadow?" were much more likely to take the top of your head off than almost any of the poems that appeared in the two Movement anthologies that had been published in 1956 and 1963.

The one poet, however, who seemed to me to have broken out of The Movement's arid confines was Thom Gunn, a writer of tightly structured but emotionally risk-taking verse who had emigrated from England and taken up residence in San Francisco in the late 1950s and who had, coincidentally, been one of my professors at Berkeley. In the classroom, Gunn would be appropriately dressed in jacket and tie, but after academic hours, I would occasionally catch sight of him outfitted in a T-shirt, jeans, black boots, and a black leather jacket, driving around the East Bay on a motorcycle. And, being both professor and motorcyclist, he wrote about bikers in the manner of an Elizabethan poet, celebrating the biker experience in his poem "On the Move," declaring that at worst, one was always in motion, and at best, "Reaching no absolute, in which to rest, / One is always nearer by not keeping still."

A few weeks after I had arrived in England, I serendipitously came across a copy of the August 3, 1967, issue of *The Listener* and was astonished to see on its front page an article by Gunn entitled "The New Music," in which this Movement poet heretically declared that songs like the Rolling Stones' "Paint It, Black," the Byrds' "Eight Miles High," Pink Floyd's "Arnold Layne," and the Beatles' "Eleanor Rigby" and "For No One" were "excellent poems—better, in fact, than many that get printed in books and magazines." Gunn further remarked on "the ordering and power that a rhythmic norm can give to a poem, a power so great that the words may survive even when the music has been lost."

The mode of the music was changing, and the walls of academe and other institutions were literally shaking. In fact, the world truly seemed to be coming untethered. It was now 1968, and many people have now forgotten about, or are too young to remember, the unparalleled social and political turbulence of that year. Both Martin Luther King and Robert F. Kennedy were assassinated. Russian troops invaded Czechoslovakia to suppress the Prague Spring. Ten days before the opening of the Summer Olympics, Mexican government troops killed an estimated two hundred students and bystanders in the Plaza de las Tres Culturas in Mexico City. Street battles between thousands of demonstrators and police, National Guardsmen, and army troops broke out at the Democratic National Convention in Chicago. In Paris, students occupied Nanterre University and the Sorbonne, and the French government appeared close to collapse after an estimated ten million of the French workforce engaged in a general strike. (One of the slogans of that day was: "The undertakers have gone on strike. Today is not a good time to die.") And in London on March 17, street fighting in front of the United States embassy in Grosvenor Square between mounted and riot police with truncheons and several thousand anti-Vietnam protesters—some throwing stones and smoke bombs—left eighty-six people injured. I myself was at that demonstration, judiciously standing at the perimeter of the square, and did a double take as I suddenly saw Mick Jagger, accompanied by several companions, rushing past me. That day's chaos was in fact the inspiration for the Rolling Stones' song "Street Fighting Man" ("Hey! Said my name is called Disturbance / I'll shout and scream, I'll kill the King, I'll rail at all his servants"). In August 1968, Chicago mayor Richard Daley forbade the city's radio stations to play that song during the Democratic National Convention; in response to the ban, the single set all-time sales records in the Chicago area.

For the first half of 1968, I was studying at the University of Essex, whose chilly plate-glass-and-steel campus was located sixty miles northeast of London, where I had weekly meetings with a professor who was supervising my studies. But in May of that year, hundreds of students initiated a massive protest aimed at halting the recruitment of students by the nearby Porton Down chemical weapons research facility where CS gas, a riot control agent then being used in Vietnam, had been developed and secretly tested. The protests grew more volatile by the day, and after three students were suspended and police with dogs were called onto the campus to restore order, nearly the entire student body voted to replace the existing university and, in its stead, declared the creation of the "Free University of Essex." I recall attending an evening rally on the campus main square and experiencing a nostalgic California moment as carousing students sang and danced to a recording of Country Joe and the Fish's anti–Vietnam War anthem "I-Feel-Like-I'm-Fixin'-to-Die Rag" ("And it's one, two, three, what are we fighting for? / Don't ask me I don't give a damn").

With classes and supervisory meetings at the university continually disrupted and canceled, I now began to wonder what *I* was studying for. Sitting one afternoon in the campus cafeteria, I happened to hear the Beatles' song "Got to Get You into My Life" playing on the radio in which Paul McCartney sang about taking a ride all alone and hoping to find "Another road where maybe I / could see another kind of mind there," and I realized that it was time for me to take the road back to London to fully embrace the role of *Rolling Stone*'s first European editor.

It was a perfect moment to do so, because in that capacity I was able to attend memorable events such as Cream's two farewell concerts at Royal Albert Hall; the now-legendary double-bill appearance of Jefferson Airplane and the Doors at London's Roundhouse (the first and last time that the Doors would ever perform in England); and the Rolling Stones' memorial tribute to Brian Jones in Hyde Park, attended by some 250,000 people, during which thousands of white butterflies were released from the stage in his honor. I spent a decidedly intoxicated weekend with Traffic's Steve Winwood, Jim Capaldi, and Chris Wood in their rustic Berkshire cottage, listening to them jam from midnight until dawn and, at the group's insistence, joining in to add a few well-received flourishes on the keyboard—even though I had never played a keyboard in my entire life! And I will never forget being present at a small dinner party given by the filmmaker John Sheppard—he had recently filmed the Doors' concert that I had attended at the Roundhouse—during which David Crosby, Stephen Stills, and Graham Nash, looking for all the world like three wayfaring cherubim, walked in unannounced, sat down at the table, and, after Stills had uncased his acoustic guitar, performed with seraphic beauty the song "Helplessly Hoping" from their still-unreleased first album.

What thrilled me most, however, was the opportunity I'd been given to interview musicians such as Mick Jagger, Pete Townshend, Ray Davies, and Syd Barrett. Only one long-harbored dream remained unfulfilled, and that was to meet my hero of heroes, the inaccessible John Lennon, who had appeared—pictured as Private Gripweed in the film *How I Won the War* and wearing his iconic round, wire-rimmed granny glasses—on the cover of *Rolling Stone*'s debut issue, which was dated November 9, 1967, with a cover price of twenty-five cents. But unbeknownst to me, destiny was about to bring that dream to fruition.

The seeds were planted when John first met Yoko exactly a year earlier. Having heard about "some amazing woman artist" who was going to be having her first solo London exhibition at the counterculture Indica Gallery, John showed up at the gallery on November 8, 1966, the evening before its official opening. "I went in," John would later tell Jann Wenner, "and I was wandering around. There were a couple of artsy-type students who had been helping, lying around there in the gallery, and I was looking at [the exhibition] and was astounded. There was an apple on sale there for two hundred quid, and I thought it was fantastic—I got the humor in her work immediately: it was two hundred quid to watch the fresh apple decompose."

The gallery owner, John Dunbar, introduced him to Yoko. "Neither of us know who the hell each other was," John said. "She didn't know who I was—she'd only heard of Ringo—I think it means 'apple' in Japanese. Dunbar insisted she say hello to the millionaire—you know what I mean. And she came up and handed me a card that said BREATHE on it—one of her instructions—so I just breathed." As Yoko later remarked, "When he breathed out, he did it really hard, and he came so near to me, it was a bit flirty in a way."

John then walked up to an artwork entitled *Painting*

to *Hammer a Nail*—a white painted wood panel with an attached hammer hanging from a chain and a box of small nails sitting next to it. John asked Yoko if she'd let him hammer in a nail, but she told him no because the exhibition's opening was not until the next day. Years later, John recalled the scene: "John Dunbar said, 'Let him hammer a nail in. He's a millionaire, he might buy it.' . . . So there was this little conference, and she finally said, 'O.K., you can hammer a nail in for five shillings,' so smart-arse here says, 'Well, I'll give you an imaginary five shillings and hammer an imaginary nail in.' And that's when we really met. That's when we locked eyes, and she got it, and I got it, and that was it.

"But it was another piece that really decided me for or against the artist: a ladder that led to a painting, which was hung on the ceiling. It looked like a black canvas with a chain with a spyglass hanging on the end of it. I climbed the ladder, looked through the spyglass, and in tiny little letters it said: YES." As John later avowed: "It was that YES that made me stay." And it was the YES at the top of the ladder that proved to be the most joyful and life-altering epiphany of his life. As he would later declare in "Mind Games"—a sermon in song that could indeed serve as his credo—"Yes is the answer, and you know that for sure. / Yes is surrender, you got to let it go."

At that time, John was married to his first wife, Cynthia, and Yoko to her second husband, the filmmaker Anthony Cox, although these marriages were fraught with tensions.

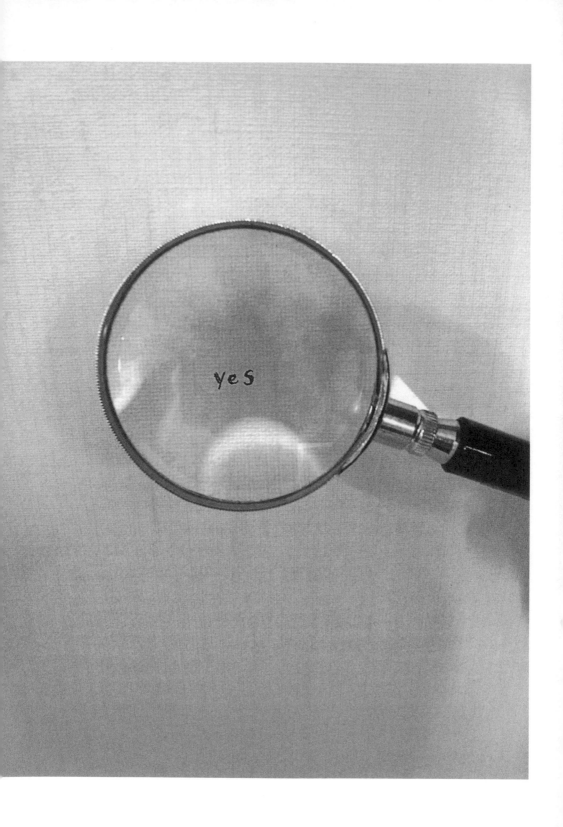

John and Yoko, whose relationship would blossom slowly, occasionally ran into each other in London. "The second time I met her," John said, "was at a gallery opening for Claes Oldenburg. We were very shy, we sort of nodded at each other. I sort of looked away because I'm very shy with people, especially chicks. We just sort of smiled and stood frozen together in this cocktail-party thing."

A short while after this second meeting, Yoko sent John a signed copy of her book *Grapefruit*—first published in 1964—which consisted of a series of mind-awakening, Zen koan–like instruction pieces and poems. John kept the book beside his bed, and at odd times he would open up the pages to read texts like: "Listen to the sound of the earth turning"; "Put your shadows together until they become one"; "Draw a line with yourself. Go on drawing until you disappear"; "Light a match and watch till it goes out"; and "Hit a wall with your head." Yoko kept John informed about her frequent events, exhibitions, and performances, so when in September 1967 she conceived of a *13 Days Do-It-Yourself Dance Festival* that took place entirely "in your mind," John received thirteen dance-instruction cards in the mail. "Different cards kept coming through the door every day," he recalled, "saying 'Breathe' and 'Dance' and 'Watch All the Lights Until Dawn,' and they upset me or made me happy, depending. I'd get very upset about it being intellectual or all fucking avant-garde, then I'd like it, and then I wouldn't."

Even after John and the other Beatles had left for India

in February 1968 to study transcendental meditation at Maharishi Mahesh Yogi's Himalayan ashram in Rishikesh, he would occasionally receive postcards from Yoko, one of which read: "Watch for me—I'm a cloud in the sky." In the fourth-century poem *The Cloud Messenger* by the Indian writer Kalidasa, an exiled lovesick demigod convinces a passing cloud to carry messages to the Himalayan home of his grieving bride; but in Yoko's case, it was *she* who was the cloud floating in the Himalayan sky above John's head, and the message she was carrying to him was *herself.* The message was received, and years later John would refer to her as Yoko in the Sky with Diamonds.

When John returned from India, one of the first things he did was to telephone Yoko. The date was May 19, 1968. "It was the middle of the night," John told Jann Wenner, "and Cynthia was away, and I thought, well, now's the time if I'm gonna get to know her any more. She came to the house and I didn't know what to do, so we went upstairs to my studio, and I played her all the tapes that I'd made, all this far-out stuff, some comedy stuff, and some electronic music. There were very few people I could play those tapes to. She was suitably impressed, and then she said, 'Well, let's make one ourselves.'"

"I was wearing a purple dress that night," Yoko would recall to the journalist Ray Connolly, "and John said later that it was a good sign because purple is a very positive color. We were very shy together at first. I mean, he just couldn't say, 'Okay, let's make it.' So he said we could either go upstairs to his studio and make some music, or stay downstairs and just chat." They went upstairs, and, as Yoko would later tell me, "it was a meeting of us through music, through making music, and it was a totally new experience for me. It just happened, it was strict improvisation, no planning. We were going into an area that none of us really knew. John was operating two tape recorders, and he was the busy one. He used everything that was around in the room—piano, organ, percussion—and I was just sitting down, doing the voice."

Recorded that night and released at the end of 1968 on the album entitled *Unfinished Music No. 1: Two Virgins*, the music begins magically with tape-looped birdcalls that function as a kind of ground bass underlying all the ensuing night's Shakespearean "noises, sounds, and sweet airs." Over snatches of saloon piano, trad jazz, and Victorian music-hall recordings, John's sound effects (reverb, delay, distortion, and white noise) mesh with Yoko's sustained keening, reminding you of the spectral sounds of a Japanese *hichiriki* pipe, as well as of the forlorn oboe lament of the duck that is swallowed by the wolf in Prokofiev's *Peter and the Wolf.* At one moment, Yoko speak-sings phrases like "Come on and make me" from a little Japanese song. Every once in a while you can overhear snatches of a conversation, as when Yoko calls out, "Is that you? Hey there!," to which John makes the grunting reply, "No fucking tin opener" and then, cheerily, "It's me

Hilda, I'm home for tea"—as if two ghost-haunted lovers in an old Japanese folktale had been transformed into a cozy British family, transfixed in the tearoom. "It was midnight when we started," John would say later. "It was dawn when we finished, and then we made love. It was very beautiful."

There was no need for Yoko to sing "Will You Still Love Me Tomorrow?" to John because, in the words of that song, the night had met the morning star, it was already tomorrow, and Yoko's heart would not be broken. Later that morning, John's oldest boyhood friend, Pete Shotton, who had been keeping him company at Kenwood for a few days, came down to the kitchen and saw John wrapped in a brown kimono-style robe making boiled eggs and tea for breakfast.

In his memoir *John Lennon: In My Life*, Shotton theatrically described the scene. "I haven't been to sleep," John announced. "I was up all night with Yoko. It was great, Pete." He then asked his friend to help him find a new house to live in, and declared that he wanted to live in it with Yoko. "Just like that?" Pete asked incredulously. "Yeah, just like that. *Just like that*," John replied. "This is *it*, Pete. This is what I've been waiting for all me life. Fuck everything else. Fuck the Beatles, fuck me money, fuck all the rest of it. I'll go and live with her in a fucking *tent* if I have to. Remember when you'd meet a girl and you'd think about her and want to be with her all the time, how your mind was just *filled* with her? Well, Yoko's upstairs now, and I can't *wait* to get back to her. I felt so hungry that I had to run down here and get meself an egg—but I can hardly bear to be away from her for a *single moment.*" And astonishingly, from that morning of May 20, 1968, until October 1973, when they separated for eighteen months, John and Yoko were rarely out of each other's sight. As John avowed in "One Day (at a Time)," perhaps his most affecting and ardent love song, "When we're together or when we're apart / There's never a space in between the beat of our hearts."

"I'd always had a fantasy about a woman who would be a beautiful, intelligent, dark-haired, high-cheek-boned, free-spirited artist (à la Juliette Gréco)," John wrote in his posthumously published book *Skywriting by Word of Mouth*. "My soul mate. Someone that I had already known, but somehow had lost. After a short visit to India on my way home from Australia, the image changed slightly—she had to be a dark-eyed *Oriental*. Naturally, the dream couldn't come true until I had completed the picture. Now it was complete."

Looking for a way to publicly announce and celebrate their union—"two minds, one destiny," as John would later characterize it—the couple accepted an invitation one month later to participate in the first National Sculpture Exhibition at Coventry Cathedral. Their contribution to the exhibition was a white, wrought-iron, circular garden bench, under which two acorns were to be planted in two white plastic pots on an east-west axis, symbolizing John and Yoko's embrace of their two respective cultures, their hopes for peace, and their love for each other. John titled the sculpture

Yoko by John—John by Yoko, and in the exhibition catalog he explained: "This is what happens when two clouds meet." One of the church canons, however, forbade the acorns to be planted on consecrated ground because John and Yoko weren't married. So the two plastic pots, like two love children, found an adoptive home in unconsecrated ground a short distance away. Within days, however, they were dug up and kidnapped by Beatle-fan zealots.

Less than a month later, John presented his first solo art exhibition in London at the Robert Fraser Gallery in Duke Street. Fraser had previously exhibited, and furthered the careers of, artists such as Jim Dine, Ed Ruscha, Peter Blake, Richard Hamilton, Bridget Riley, and Andy Warhol. In the mid-sixties, the Robert Fraser Gallery served as a salon for writers, actors, and musicians like Dennis Hopper, William Burroughs, Marianne Faithfull, Mick Jagger, and Keith Richards. A man of wealth and taste, Fraser, who died in 1986, achieved notoriety when he was arrested in 1967, along with Jagger and Richards, in an infamous drug bust during a party at Richards's Sussex home. Although Jagger and Richards were acquitted on appeal, Fraser was sentenced to six months in prison.

John's exhibition opened on July 1, 1968, when Fraser was once again a free man. The title of John's show, which he dedicated to Yoko, was *You Are Here*, a reference to the maps on the boards that John used to see in Liverpool's parks when he was a child. I attended the star-studded opening, and as I entered the gallery, I observed 365 white balloons being filled with helium on the main floor. Attached to the balloons were tags printed with the words "You Are Here" on one side and, on the other "Write to John Lennon c/o Robert Fraser Gallery, 69 Duke Street, London W1." John explained that as a child he found a tagged balloon from Australia, and it pleased him so much that he decided to imitate the idea. He and Yoko were dressed completely in white in order to chime with both the gallery's white walls and the white circular eight-foot-diameter canvas mounted in the basement in whose center John had written "you are here" in tiny letters. Later, all the attendees congregated outside, and John released the balloons into the London sky as he announced: "I declare these balloons . . . high!"

The responses to the found balloon tags that were mailed back to the gallery, as well as comment left in the gallery's guest book, were occasionally amiable and complimentary, and even included a witty poem or weighty statement to ponder ("Whispering brutality justifies the sun to falter in reality"). But the majority of the messages were sarcastic and abusive toward John ("Long hairred spectical faced turt"; "Best wishes for a speedy recovery"; "Go back to your wife, she loves you"; "Mickey Mouse loves you, so it's alright") and virulent and racist with regard to Yoko. John was particularly devastated by these attacks directed at the woman whom he called his "goddess of love and the fulfillment of my whole life." But in *Skywriting by Word of Mouth*, John reflected: "Having been brought up in the genteel poverty of a lower-middle-class environment, I should not have been surprised by the outpouring of race-hatred and anti-female malice to which we were subjected in that bastion of democracy, Great Britain. What a riot! One of 'our boys' leaving his Anglo-Saxon (whatever that is) hearth and home and taking up with a bloody Jap to boot! Doesn't he know about *The Bridge on the River Kwai*? Doesn't he remember Pearl Harbor? . . . The press led the howling mob, and the foul-mouthed Silent Majority followed suit."

Shortly after Yoko had become John's lover and collaborator, a young girl approached her outside Abbey Road Studios and handed her a bouquet of yellow roses, thorns first. One London journalist asserted that Yoko was "the most vilified woman in the world." But as Yoko herself remarked to *Playboy*'s David Sheff, "When all that hate energy was focused on me, it was transformed into a fantastic energy. It was supporting me. If you are centered and you can transform all this energy that comes in, it will help you. If you believe it is going to kill you, it will kill you."

But Yoko wasn't hated at that time simply for being with John. Many people also lambasted her artistic endeavors and assumed that she was somehow "bringing him down" into her own conceptual and avant-garde gravitational field. What these disparagers didn't realize was that before John had even heard of or encountered Yoko, he had been engaging in sonic experiments of his own in his home recording studio—playing tapes backward, altering their speeds, recording and manipulating sound fragments, and deconstructing and transforming tunes into sound collages and novel soundscapes. "When I first met John," Yoko once told me, "he played me some of the cassette tapes that he used to make in the hotel rooms where he was staying when he was touring with the Beatles. Like one time in Japan he recorded himself mumbling something, and then he'd turn on the radio and there would be a voice speaking Japanese, and he'd record that too so that it became a dialogue between the radio and him. He didn't know about the avant-garde, he was just doing it for fun."

But even in those dark days, Yoko refused to lose faith, preferring to look at the bright side of things. I had a chance to sit down with her one afternoon to ask her how she was managing to deal with those whom I snobbishly and intolerantly referred to as the "uncomprehending nitwits" who refused to make an effort to understand what she and John were trying to do with their music, films, exhibitions, and performance events. But Yoko was much more charitable than I. "I actually don't think there *are* any nitwits," she gently disagreed with me. "I've recently begun to think about all of this, and I now realize that the avant-garde intellectuals are saying, 'Oh, the establishment is always going to be there, there are always going to be nitwits, you're not going to be able to really fight them, they're always going to call you stupid.' But I don't believe that. Like if you once know something—and this is a natural law—you can never *unknow* it. If you're once raped, you're never going to be a virgin again. The point is that artists are very much a part of society, they're not separate from it. And what they're trying to do is to sort of engage in a vast scale of *intellectual* rape, in a way, of the entire population. But I want to explain that by 'rape' I only mean that people will have their minds opened and will therefore be able to free themselves from their limited preconceptions. And that's great because once all the doors will be open, you'll never be able to close them again. And then people will have to open *themselves* up and learn to become receptive, and therefore be able to understand and communicate. I think that this is going to happen rapidly, and I really believe that the total appreciation I'm talking about will come soon."

A week before John's *You Are Here* exhibition was going to close, I revisited the Robert Fraser Gallery to see the show one last time. On the afternoon I was there, I decided to introduce myself to Fraser, whom I found surprisingly approachable and gracious. He told me that he subscribed to *Rolling Stone,* and when I mentioned that I would love to interview John for the magazine, he informed me that the Beatles were in the midst of working on their *White Album,* and that he doubted that John would have time to see me. But he took down my phone number and said that he'd propose the idea to him and would report back if he heard something positive. At the end of August, I received my dreamed-of call. Fraser conveyed to me the news that John was willing to grant me an interview in mid-September, and offered to act as liaison with regard to arranging all the details. A week later, Fraser phoned to tell me that I should come to John and Yoko's London flat on September 17 at five o'clock in the afternoon and that he would be there as well to make the introductions.

John had recently moved out of his Kenwood home, and he and Yoko, who had recently separated from their respective spouses, set up temporary residence at 34 Montagu Square in Marylebone—their first domicile as a couple and one that now displays an English Heritage blue plaque to commemorate John's sojourn there in 1968. It is a place, moreover, that has accrued additional legendary status as a rock-'n'-roll mecca because of some of the other luminaries whom it had previously lodged.

In 1965, Ringo Starr had leased this basement-and-ground-floor flat shortly before his marriage to Maureen Cox. When informed by a journalist that the Beatles' drummer would be moving into the neighborhood, a resident named Lord Mancroft remarked: "We're a very distinguished square, and I'm sure we'll welcome such a distinguished gentleman with his lady." Ringo and Maureen, however, lived in the square for only a month. They bought and immediately moved into a country house in Surrey, but Ringo held on to his lease.

In 1966, he rented the flat to Paul McCartney who transformed the basement into a mini–recording studio where he made a demo of his song "I'm Looking Through You" and also began to compose "Eleanor Rigby." But Paul had originally intended the studio to be a place where poets and musicians could create spoken-word and avant-garde works for the short-lived but ambitious Zapple Records, a subsidiary of Apple Records. Only two albums, however, were released by the label before it folded—John and Yoko's *Unfinished Music No. 2: Life with the Lions* and George Harrison's *Electronic Sound*—although three other albums of readings by the American writers Richard Brautigan, Lawrence Ferlinghetti, and Michael McClure had previously been recorded.

Realizing that the studio was being underused, Paul dismantled it and gave up the flat, and it remained empty until December 1966 when Ringo decided to sublet it to Jimi Hendrix; Hendrix's manager, Chas Chandler; and their respective girlfriends. This would not prove to be one of Ringo's shrewder moves. Hendrix and his then-girlfriend, Kathy Etchingham, moved into the flat's basement. One night, in a domestic dispute that has now become a legendary episode in the annals of rock 'n' roll, Hendrix made a quite undiplomatic after-dinner remark to Etchingham that pointedly raised questions about her cooking prowess, which resulted in her hurling plates, utensils, glasses, pots, and pans about the kitchen before storming out of the flat to spend the night at the home of Eric Burdon, the lead vocalist of the Animals. In despair, Hendrix sat down and wrote one of his most affecting songs, "The Wind Cries Mary," in which he laments "The traffic lights they turn up blue tomorrow / And shine their emptiness down on my bed," as the wind, in the song's chorus, whispers, screams, and cries "Mary"—Etchingham's middle name. Not long thereafter, Hendrix—while on LSD—trashed the flat and, perhaps under the unconscious influence of a Rolling Stones song, decided that it would be an inspired idea to paint the walls black, though an alternative, less likely story has Hendrix throwing whitewash over the walls. In either case, Ringo was soon looking for a new tenant.

I arrived at 34 Montagu Square on Tuesday, September 17, 1968, at five o'clock in the afternoon. I nervously rang the doorbell, and after a few seconds, a smiling John Lennon—his round, wire-rimmed granny glasses immediately gave him away—opened the door. "Come in, come in!" he said, took my coat, then led me into the living room where I saw Robert Fraser sitting on a couch next to Yoko Ono, who was dressed in a black sweater and black pants. Glancing around the room, I was instantly transfixed by the astonishing array of photos and posters hanging on the walls. Among them were the two full-length nude photos of John and Yoko that would appear on the controversial cover of their soon-to-be-released *Unfinished Music No. 1: Two Virgins* album; a giant Sgt. Pepper ensign; the fanciful 1967 *Time* magazine Beatles cover for which the cartoonist Gerald Scarfe had sculpted the group using papier-mâché,

paste, wire, sticks, and watercolors; and Richard Hamilton's iconic poster collage made up of news clippings about the Rolling Stones' 1967 drug bust, for which Fraser had received his six-month prison sentence. There was the scent of Indian incense in the air, and John, Yoko, Robert, and I sat down around a simple wooden table covered with magazines, newspapers, a beaded necklace shaped in the form of a pentacle, a sketch pad on which I caught a glimpse of some of John's inimitable skittery cartoonlike drawings, and an ashtray brimming over with French Gitanes cigarette butts.

We began talking about John's recent *You Are Here* exhibition but were shortly interrupted by the ringing of the telephone. John got up to take the call, and when he returned, he informed me apologetically that he'd just found out that he needed to be at an all-night Beatles recording session at Abbey Road Studios for the *White Album*. So we agreed to meet up the next day to do the interview. But as I got up to leave, John unexpectedly said, "Why don't you just come along with Yoko and me to the session."

"Right now? Are you sure it's O.K.?" I asked him disbelievingly.

"Of course, of course, no worry," he replied without hesitation.

John, Yoko, and I left the flat, entered a waiting limousine, and were driven to St. John's Wood. Little did I know, as we got out of the car and walked over the pedestrian zebra crossing into Abbey Road Studios, that we were actually tra-

versing sacred ground, for that crossing would eventually become a pilgrimage site for Beatles fans throughout the world. And for an undeservedly blessed fan like myself, making my way into Abbey Road Studio Two was like entering into the Holy of Holies. But because I was John's unworthy, interloping guest, it was hardly surprising when the other three musical evangelists, swerving around on their stools as I made my appearance, greeted me with Medusa-like stares. So I immediately decided to make myself scarce behind one of the giant studio speakers and remained standing there for the next several hours.

Beatles recording sessions were always an amalgam of rehearsing, jamming, laying down tracks, mixing and remixing, overdubbing, double-tracking, adding and layering voices, creating sound effects, and unceasing editing. I will always imagine that what I entered into that night was a Mid-Autumn Night's Dream, one inhabited by both angels and devils, and filled with Shakespearean sweet airs, noises, and a thousand twangling instruments that at various times in my lucid dream were either humming or screaming in my ears.

On that night's session I first listened to the sweet airs of John's song "Glass Onion," in which his mythologizing stream of consciousness flowed gently through fields of strawberries where walruses, fools on a hill, and lady madonnas had forgathered in the singer's dreaming mind. But sweet dream turned into nightmare as "Glass Onion" segued into the "madness and hysterics"—as Ringo described it—of Paul's uncharacteristically apocalyptic, proto-metal song "Helter Skelter." As Paul explained it: "We deliberately decided to do the loudest, nastiest, sweatiest rock number we could." He succeeded, and it was this song from hell that woke me from my dream. But when I did awaken, I found myself still standing in the seventh heaven of Abbey Road Studios, and realized that everything was real and that I really had been at a Beatles recording session. Only my attending a rehearsal for a Shakespeare play at the Globe Theatre might have made me feel as imparadised as I did that night.

On the following afternoon, September 18, I returned to Montagu Square. Yoko opened the front door and led me into the living room where I observed John walking aimlessly around the room as if in a kind of daydream, half humming and half singing the Beatles' "Hold Me Tight" as if to the air ("Tell me I'm the only one / And then, I might never be the lonely one"). After about fifteen seconds, John turned around, stopped singing, and, in the words of an old song, saw me standing there.

"Did you stay long last night at the recording session?" John asked me. "When did you leave?"

"Just before midnight," I told him. "One of the Abbey Road people said it was time for me to go."

"Yeh, it went on really late," John said, "and Yoko and I only had two hours' sleep, I'm not quite here yet. So I need to listen to a few songs before we start the interview."

Yoko told us that she was going to rest for a while in the bedroom and would see us later. When she left, John plopped down on the floor. Old 45 rpm records were scattered everywhere, and deciding to play DJ, John picked up three or four of them, stood up, and put the first of the 45s—Gene Vincent's 1956 rockabilly song "Woman Love"—on the turntable. As we started listening to it, John remarked: "I used to play this over and over in the old days but couldn't ever understand the words . . . like these words here right now . . . what are they saying?" In spite of the recording's slap-back echo, I took a stab at it: "It sounds like 'Well I'm lookin' for a woman with a one track mind / A-fuggin' and a-kissin' and a-smoochin' all the time.' " (The lyric sheet says "a-huggin' " not "a-fuggin'," but the singer was obviously having it both ways.) "Yeh," John said, "I loved this song, and of course Gene's 'Be-Bop-A-Lula,' too.

"Now listen to this one," John insisted, as he played me the next song—Rosie and the Originals' 1960 version of "Give Me Love." "This is really one of the greatest strange records," he remarked. "It's all just out of beat, and everyone misses it. The A side was the hit, 'Angel Baby'—which is one of my favorite songs—and they knocked off the B side in ten minutes. I'm always talking Yoko's ear off, telling her about these songs, saying, 'Look, this is *this*!' and 'This is *this* . . . and *this* . . . and *this*!'

"And now listen to *this*," John said passionately, "this is the last song I'll play you." And out of the speakers came the deliquescent sounds of Smokey Robinson and the Miracles' "I've Been Good to You," a song from 1961 that provides the melody and chords for the Beatles' "This Boy," and whose opening lines of voluptuous torment—"Look what you've done / You made a fool out of someone"—were the specific inspiration for "Sexy Sadie" ("Sexy Sadie, what have you done? / You made a fool of everyone"). "Smokey Robinson has the most *perfect* voice," John declared, as he began singing along with and imitating Smokey's swooning vocal line with its gospel curlicues and flowers and frills [*singing falsetto*]: " 'You know that you're hurting me so—oh—oh—oh—oh—oh—ohhh . . .'—no breath! A beautiful piece."

"What an incredible song!" I said as he turned off the phonograph. "That's really an astonishing vocal performance."

"I know," he agreed. "I go wild every time I hear it."

John again sat down on the living-room floor, and I walked over to the chair where I'd left my shoulder bag, took out my cassette recorder and a little notebook filled with questions, and then also sat down, somewhat nervously, across from him. "Don't worry, don't worry," John assured me. "There's nothing more fun than talking about your own songs and your own records. I mean, you can't help it, it's your bit, really. And we talk about them together. Remember that."

"Thanks," I said, feeling more relaxed. "If you don't mind—"

"Everything's O.K.," John reminded me. "Just ask me what you'd like to know."

"O.K.," I began, "I'd actually like to start out asking you about some of the songs that I've always associated with you, in terms of what you are or what you were—songs that strike me as embodying you a little bit."

"Which ones?" John asked.

"I made a little list of them: 'You've Got to Hide Your Love Away,' 'Strawberry Fields Forever,' 'It's Only Love,' 'She Said She Said,' 'Lucy in the Sky with Diamonds,' 'I'm Only Sleeping,' 'Run for Your Life,' 'I Am the Walrus,' 'All You Need Is Love,' 'Rain,' 'Girl.'"

"Yeh," John said, then paused for a moment. "I agree with some of them. 'Hide Your Love Away'—right, I'd just discovered Dylan, really. 'It's Only Love'—I was always ashamed of that because of the abominable lyrics."

"Abominable lyrics? That song is really one from the heart!"

"Yeh, the lyrics are probably all right," John conceded. "But you know, George came over just the other night, and for some reason we were actually talking about that song, and he said, 'You remember, we all used to *cringe* when the guitar bit came on: *Blah-de-la-la-lah.*' There was something wrong with it, you know . . . And 'She Said She Said'—yeh, I dug that because I was going through a bad time writing then. But then I heard it and so I dug it. 'Lucy in the Sky,' 'I'm Only Sleeping'—O.K., it's like that. 'Run for Your

Life' I always hated. 'Walrus,' yeh. 'Rain,' yeh. 'Girl,' yeh. 'All You Need Is Love'—hah, that's sort of natural. 'Ticket to Ride' was another, I remember that. It was a definite sort of change. But the ones that really mean something to me—they're probably 'She Said She Said,' 'Walrus,' 'Rain,' 'Norwegian Wood,' 'Girl,' and 'Strawberry Fields.' I consider them moods or moments. It's the 'me' touch, and I'll sort of stick me name on them."

"Someone," I said, "once told me that 'Strawberry Fields' was written when you were sitting on a beach somewhere. Is that true?"

"It was in Spain when I was filming *How I Won the War* for six weeks last year," John recalled. "I was going through a big scene about songwriting again—I seem to go through it now and then. And it took me a long time to write 'Strawberry Fields.' I was writing it in bits and bits and bits, and I wanted the lyrics to be the way you and I are talking now, like *talkingIjusthappentobesinging*—just like that. Part of it was written in a big Spanish home, and then finished on the beach. It was really romantic, singing it to . . . I don't know who was there."

"Don't you think there's something special about that song? The way you describe your mind ebbing and flowing like an ocean is pretty amazing."

"Yeh, definitely, it was a big scene. Like 'Rain' was a big scene because it was the time I discovered *backwards* accidentally."

"Backwards?" I said. "What's backwards?"

"At the end of 'Rain,' " John explained, "you hear me singing backwards."

"What did backwards sound like?" I asked him.

"It sounded something like [*sings*] *writherinignthawathin*—like that. We'd recorded the main part at EMI Studios, and the habit then was for us to take the tape of what we'd recorded back home with us and see what little extra gimmick or guitar bit we could add. So I got home, stoned out of me head, staggered up to me tape recorder, put my earphones on, and I just happened to put the tape in the wrong way round, and the song just came out *backwards*. I was in a trance in the earphones—*what is it? what is it?* It was too *much*, you know, it just blew me mind, it was fantastic, it sounded like some kind of Indian music. And I just really wanted the *whole* song to be backwards. But instead we just tagged it onto the end."

"A lot of my friends," I told him, "like to sit around analyzing your songs."

"Well, they *can* take them apart. They can take anything apart."

"And you don't mind that?"

"Surely not. I mean, I hit it on all levels, you know. I write lyrics, and you don't realize what they mean till after. Especially some of the better songs or some of the more flowing ones, like 'Walrus.' The whole first verse was written without any knowledge. And 'Tomorrow Never Knows'—I didn't know what I was saying, and you just find out later. It's really just like abstract art. When you have to think about it to write it, it just means that you've labored at it. But when you just *say* it, man, it's a continuous flow. The same as when you're recording or just playing—you come out of a thing and you know *'I've been there'*—it's just pure, and that's what we're really looking for all the time. So when there are some lyrics of mine that I dig, I know that somewhere people will be looking at them. And so the people who analyze the songs—good on 'em, because they work on all levels. So I don't mind what they do with them."

"Whenever I listen to 'Strawberry Fields,' " I confessed, "I like to do so with my eyes closed and make up little fantasies about it. But what *is* Strawberry Fields?"

"It's a name," John said. "It's a nice name. When I was writing 'In My Life,' I was trying to write about Liverpool, and I just started listing a lot of nice-sounding Liverpool names, just arbitrarily."

"Just places that you remembered?" I wondered.

"Yeh. Strawberry Fields was a place near us that happened to be a Salvation Army home. But Strawberry Fields—I mean, I have visions of *strawberry fields*. And there was Penny Lane, and the Cast Iron Shore [a name given to the banks of the River Mersey in south Liverpool] which I've just put in my new song 'Glass Onion.' They were just good names, just groovy names."

"I've always felt," I added, "that songs like 'Good Morning Good Morning' and 'Penny Lane' suggest in such a beautiful way a child's feeling of the world. I wonder if you feel that way too."

"Yeh," John agreed, "because we write about our past. 'Good Morning Good Morning'—I was never proud of it, I just knocked it off to do a song. But it does get that kid thing because when I was writing it, it *was* me at school. The same with 'Penny Lane.' We really got into the groove of imagining Penny Lane—the bank was there, and that was where the tram sheds were and people waiting and the inspector stood there, the fire engines were down there. It was just reliving childhood."

"You really had a place where you grew up," I said with a touch of envy.

"Oh, yeh. Didn't you?" he said with surprise.

"Well, Manhattan isn't Liverpool."

"Well, you could write about your local bus station," John suggested.

"My local bus station? In Manhattan?"

"Sure," John said. "Why not? Everywhere is somewhere. And Strawberry Fields is anywhere you want to go."

"I think I'd have preferred to live near Penny Lane," I told him, "where the pretty miss is selling poppies from a tray."

"Pretty *nurse!*" John corrected me.

"Whoops, right. The pretty *nurse* is selling poppies from a tray—'And though she feels as if she's in a play / She is anyway.' I've always loved those lines. It reminds me of a little kid singing about what's happening on a bright sunny day. But there's also that sense of playing with the idea about what's real and what's not real—as if *everything* is in fact a play."

"Yeh," John replied. "Paul had the main bit of that, but I remember working on those lines, too. And it's always been a bit of 'She's in a play, she is anyway—heh, heh.' Because it's a *game*, man, it's a game—it's all right, and everything's O.K. So there *is* all that in it. But to us it's just Penny Lane because we lived there."

"When I was at the recording session last night," I mentioned to him, "I started drifting in and out of consciousness for a little while, and at one point I could swear that I heard you singing about strawberry fields and walruses and fools on the hill—it was all just blending together."

"Yeh, we were working part of the time on 'Glass Onion,' " John explained, "and I was singing, 'I told you 'bout Strawberry Fields, you know the place where nothing is real' . . . and then I was singing, 'I told you 'bout the walrus and me, man, you know that we're as close as can be, man' . . . and then I was singing, 'I told you 'bout the fool on the hill, I tell you, man, he living there still.' You heard it right."

"Do you think that you're all trying consciously to construct a kind of Beatles myth?" I asked him. "You seem to have been doing that with *Sgt. Pepper, Yellow Submarine*, and *Magical Mystery Tour*."

"Yeh, we got a bit pretentious," John admitted. "Like everybody, we had our phase, and now we're trying to be more natural, less 'newspaper taxis,' say. I mean, we're changing. I don't know what we're doing at all, I just write them. Really, I just like rock 'n' roll. I mean, those records I played you before"—and John now pointed to the pile of 45s on the floor—"I dug them *then*, I dig them *now*, and I'm still trying to reproduce 'Some Other Guy' or 'Be-Bop-A-Lula.' Whatever it is. It's just the sound."

"I wanted to ask you, John, about something that's always charmed me about the way the Beatles make a distinction between lovers and friends."

"In what sense?" John asked.

"Well, there's the 'baby' who can drive your car, but in 'We Can Work It Out,' the song says that life's very short and there's no time for 'fussing and fighting, my friend.' And in 'All Together Now,' it's not 'baby let me follow you down' but rather 'A, B, C, D, can I bring my friend to tea?' "

"I know what you mean," John said, "but I don't know why. It's Paul's bit, that—'Buy you a diamond ring, my friend'—it's an alternative to 'baby.' You can take it logically the way you took it. See, I don't know really. Yours is as true a way of looking at it as any other way. In 'Baby You're a Rich Man,' the point was: Stop moaning, you're a rich man and we're all rich men, heh heh, baby!"

"It's also a bit of a mocking song, isn't it?"

"Well, they all get like that 'cause there *is* all that in

them," he explained, "and that's the point. Because as we sing them, that *happens*. In different takes, just the intonation of your voice will change the meaning of the lyrics. And that's why it's *after* we've done them that we really see what it was, because by that time the weight's on them."

"When 'All You Need Is Love' was first released," I mentioned, "I was at a swimming pool in California one afternoon, and someone there had a radio on that was playing that song. And this nine- or ten-year-old girl started singing along, but instead of saying 'All you need is love,' she started laughing and shouting out 'All you need is hate.' That really gave me the willies."

"Could be right, you know," John responded with a grim laugh. "But when I wrote the song I meant *love*, I felt that's what you needed. But when I'm down, it doesn't work at all, though I believe it in the songs. So I write: All you need is love, there you go! It's just that you can't always live up to it."

"Recently," I admitted to John, "I've been feeling another one of your moods—'Here I stand, head in hand / Turn my face to the wall'—and also the mood of your song 'She Said She Said,' in which some girl is making you feel like you've never been born."

"That was pure," John told me. "That was what I meant all right. You see, when I wrote that, I had the 'She said she said,' but it was just meaning nothing. It had something vaguely to do with someone who had said something like he knew what it was like to be dead. It was just a sound. The beginning of the song had been around for days and days, and then I just decided to write down the first thing that came into my head, and it was 'When I was a boy, everything was right' in a different beat, but it was real because it just happened. It's funny, but while we're recording, we're all aware of our old records, and we're even listening to our old records, and sometimes we'll say, Let's do one like 'The Word,' make it like that. It never really does turn out that way, but we're always comparing and talking about the old albums—just checking up, like swotting up for the exam—just listening to everything we've done."

"Some people," I noted, "think that in songs like 'You've Got to Hide Your Love Away' and 'She Said She Said' you were turning your back on the kind of fifties rock-'n'-roll songs that you were playing to me before. Do you think they have a point?"

"Yeh, yeh, we got completely involved in ourselves then. I think that it was *Rubber Soul* when we did all our own numbers. Something just happened, and we tried to control it a little bit. But you know, I'd still like to make a record like 'Some Other Guy.' I haven't done one that satisfies me as much as that satisfied me. Or 'Be-Bop-A-Lula' or 'Heartbreak Hotel' or 'Good Golly Miss Molly' or 'Whole Lotta Shakin' Goin' On.'"

"I beg to disagree," I said. "I think you're really being overly modest."

"But I'm not being modest at all," he answered. "I mean,

we're still trying it. We sit there in the studio and we say, 'How did that old song go, how did it go? Come on let's do *that.*' Like what Fats Domino has done with 'Lady Madonna'—'See how they ruhhnnn.' That's a groove."

"Are there any other versions of your songs that you like?" I asked.

"Well, Ray Charles's version of 'Yesterday'—that's beautiful. And his 'Eleanor Rigby' is a groove. I just dig the strings on that. Like thirties strings. José Feliciano does great things to 'Help!' and 'Day Tripper.' And I think that Judy Collins's 'In My Life' is quite nice."

"I've got to tell you, John, that when I first heard the Beatles' 'Got to Get You into My Life,' I immediately thought of Tamla Motown."

"Sure," he agreed, "we were doing our Tamla Motown bit. You see, we're influenced by whatever's going on. Even if we're not influenced, we're all going that way at a certain time. If we played a Stones record now, and then a Beatles record—and we've been way apart—you'd find a lot of similarities. We're all heavy. Just heavy. How did we ever do anything light? But what we're trying to do now is rock 'n' roll, with less of your philoso-rock, is what we're saying to ourselves. And just get on with rocking, because rockers is what we really are. You can give me a guitar, stand me up in front of a few people, and that's what I am. Even in the studio, if I'm getting into it, I'm just doing my old bit—not quite doing Elvis legs but doing my equivalent. It's just natural.

Everybody says we must do this and that, but our thing is rocking. And that's what our new record is about. Definitely rocking. What we were doing on *Pepper* was rocking—and not rocking."

"When people think of *Sgt. Pepper*," I observed, "they usually think of 'A Day in the Life' as being its high point. Do you?"

"Yeh, 'A Day in the Life' was something," John agreed. "I dug it. It was a good piece of work between Paul and me. I had the 'I read the news today, oh boy' bit, and it turned Paul on. Now and then we really turn each other on with a bit of a song, and he just said, 'Yeh!' And then it all just sort of happened beautifully—bang, bang, like that—and we arranged it and rehearsed it, which we don't often do, the afternoon before we were going to record it. So we all knew what we were playing, and we all got into it. It was a real groove, the whole scene, on that one. Paul sang half of it and I sang half. I needed a middle eight, but that would have been forcing it. All the rest of the song had come out smooth, flowing, no trouble, and fortunately Paul already had a middle eight—'Woke up, fell out of bed / Dragged a comb across my head.' "

"Along with Jimi Hendrix's version of 'The Star-Spangled Banner' that he performed at Woodstock," I remarked to John, " 'A Day in the Life' has got to be the most apocalyptic, end-of-days rock song of all time."

"Yeh, it's a bit of a *2001*, you know."

"One critic," I told him, "described 'A Day in the Life' as being like a kind of miniature *The Waste Land*."

"Miniature what?" John asked.

"T. S. Eliot's poem *The Waste Land*."

"What's it about?"

"Part of it takes place in rats' alley," I explained, "where the dead men have lost their bones—it's like an early version of Dylan's 'Desolation Row.' And it's really ironical that in Dylan's song, he actually sings 'And Ezra Pound and T. S. Eliot / Fighting in the captain's tower!' "

"Don't know that T. S. Eliot poem," John admitted. "I'm not very hip on me culture, you know."

"So you don't think, as some people do, that 'A Day in the Life' was some kind of peak?"

"Well, I actually think that whatever we're doing now is past what we were doing then, even if there's no one song comparable to it. It was only a song, and it turned out well. But there are plenty more."

"I just bought the new Beatles' single, 'Hey Jude,' " I told him, "and in a way it sounds to me like a person who's singing to someone else but also to himself."

"Both. Both," John agreed. "When Paul first played the little tape of 'Hey Jude' to me, I took it very personally. 'Ah, it's me!' And Paul said, 'No, it's me!' And I said, 'Check, we're going through the same thing.' So whoever is going through that bit with us is also going through it. That's the groove."

"A friend of mine," I mentioned, "said to me that the end of 'Hey Jude' sounded to him a little bit like a mantra. Do you think so too?"

"I never thought about that," John said, "and it was nothing conscious, but it could have been. As I said to you before, it's all valid. I mean, we'd recently come back from India. But I always related it to some Drifters' song, or the Stones' 'You Better Move On,' or Sam Cooke's 'Send Me Some Lovin'.' "

"I've noticed that millions of Beatles fans seem to want to send some lovin' to all of you all of the time," I joked. "And I've always thought there's something really endearing about the way the Beatles are always singing about how they're 'hoping' and 'dying' to 'take us away.' On *Sgt. Pepper* you all sing 'We'd like to take you home with us,' and in 'Hey Bulldog,' you yourself propose that 'If you're lonely you can talk to me.' So I was curious to know how you balance this come-sit-on-my-lawn feeling with your own need for privacy."

"The concept is very good," John replied, "and I actually went through that and said, 'Well, okay, let them sit on my lawn.' But then people just climb in the house and smash things up, and you think, 'That's no good, that's not going to work.' So actually you wind up saying, *Don't* talk to me, really. We're all trying to say nice things, but ninety percent of the time we can't make it, and the odd time that we do make it work is when we're all doing it *together* as people. And you can say that in a song. So whatever I might have said to someone that day about getting out of my garden, a *part* of me said that, but, really, in my heart of hearts, I *would* like to communicate and talk with him or her. But unfortunately we're human, you know."

"It's been four years since your album *Meet the Beatles* was first released in America," I said, "and everyone was, to say the least, pleased to meet all of you. Are you still pleased with your early albums?"

"You know, I was just recently listening to *Please Please Me* again, and it's embarrassing . . . and nice . . . but it was embarrassing even then, because we knew what we wanted it to be like but didn't know how to do it in the studio, we didn't have the knowledge or the experience. But some of it's sweet, it's all right, you know. In the early days I'd—well, we all did—we'd take things out for being banal, and there were even chords we wouldn't use because we thought they were clichés. But just this year there's been a great release for all of us, because we're going right back to the basics. On my song 'Revolution' I'm playing the guitar, and it sounds the way I want it to sound. It's a pity I can't do better fingering, you know. But I couldn't have done that last year, I'd have been too paranoiac."

"Paranoiac?" I said, surprised.

"It usually is the case," he added with a laugh. "Lost paranoias."

"But what do you mean when you say you were paranoiac about your fingering?"

"What I mean is that I didn't think that I could play *d-d-d-d-d-d-d-d-d-d-d.* George had to play that, or somebody better than me. I was always the rhythm guy anyway, but I didn't actually want to play rhythm. We all sort of wanted to be lead—as in most groups—but it's a groove now, and so are the clichés. And also we've gone past those days when we wouldn't have used words because they didn't make sense, or what we thought was sense. But of course Dylan taught us a lot in that regard. And another thing is, I used to write a book or stories on one hand and write songs on the other. And I'd be writing completely free-form in a book, but when I'd start to write a song I'd be thinking *dee-duh dee-duh doo / do-de do-de doo.* And it took Dylan, and all that was going on then, for me to say, Oh, come on now, it's the same bit, I can just *sing* the words."

"Like what you did with 'I Am the Walrus'?"

"With 'I Am the Walrus,' " John said, "I had the first two lines on the typewriter—'I am he as you are he as you are me and we are all together' and 'See how they run like pigs from a gun, see how they fly.' And then about two weeks later I wrote another two lines, and then I just knocked the rest of it off and sang it. I had this idea of doing a song that was like a police siren, but it didn't work in the end." At this point John started wailing like a siren: "IAMHEAS-YOUAREHEAS . . . But you can't really sing a police siren."

"I've always wondered, John, what you thought of Dylan's 'take' on 'Norwegian Wood' in his song 'Fourth Time Around'?"

"I was very paranoiac about that, *too*," John told me. "I remember that Dylan played it to me when he was in London. He said, 'What do you think?' I said, 'I don't like it.' I didn't like it. I just didn't like what I *felt* I was feeling—I thought it was an out-and-out skit, you know, but it was and it wasn't. I mean, he wasn't playing any tricks on me."

"I've noticed that a lot of people seem to associate you with Dylan in some way, as if the two of you were somehow connected both musically and personally."

"Yeh? Really? Yeh, well we were for a bit," John said. "I always saw him when he was in London, but I couldn't make it. Like I said, too paranoiac. He was the first one to turn us on in New York actually. He thought that 'I Want to Hold Your Hand'—when it goes 'I can't hide'—he thought we were singing 'I get high,' you see. So he turns up and turns us on, and we had the biggest laugh all night—forever. Fantastic. We've got a lot to thank him for. If I was in New York, he'd be the person I'd most like to see. I may have grown up enough to communicate with him. Both of us were always uptight, you know, and of course I wouldn't know whether he was uptight, because I was so uptight. And then, when he wasn't uptight, I was. But we just sat it out because we liked being together."

"What do you think of his more relaxed country-sounding new music?"

"Dylan broke his neck, and we went to India. Everybody went through that, and now we're all just coming out, coming out of a shell, in a new way, kind of saying, remember what it was like to play."

"Do you feel better now?" I asked.

"Yes . . . and worse," he replied with a laugh.

"What are your feelings now about the time you spent in India?"

"I've got no regrets at all," he told me, "because it was a groove and I had some great experiences meditating eight hours a day—some amazing things, some amazing trips—it was great. The song 'Mother Nature's Son' is typically India. And I still meditate off and on. George is doing it regularly. And I believe implicitly in the whole thing. It's just that it's difficult to continue it, and I also lost the rosy glasses. And I'm like that, I'm very idealistic, and I can't really manage me exercises when I've lost that. It's just that a few things happened, or didn't happen. I don't know, but *something* happened. It was sort of like a"—John snapped his fingers—"and we just left."

At that moment, John asked me if I happened to know what time it was, so I looked at my watch, told him that it was six thirty, and John said, "I've got a bit more time to finish up our interview, Jonathan, but Yoko and I have to leave for Abbey Road in about an hour." I asked him what song the Beatles would be working on that night, and John said they hadn't planned anything at all, but they'd probably come up with something or other. I later found out that Paul, who had gotten to the studio early, was already playing around with a guitar riff when John, George, and Ringo arrived, and, with that riff as their inspiration, they all began jamming. John and Paul made up some lyrics on the spot about how they'd heard it was someone's birthday—they apparently had no one's birthday in mind—and that they hoped it was going to be a happy one . . . and that it was surprisingly *their* birthday too, and that they were all going to party and have a really good time! They invited Yoko and George's wife, Pattie Boyd, to join in with backing vocals and handclaps, and after twenty takes—and before the night was through—they had created the song "Birthday."

"O.K.," John told me, "I'm going to make both of us some tea and then we can talk a little more." He got up and went to the kitchen. Glancing at the walls, my eyes were immediately drawn to two photos that I'd noticed when I first arrived at the flat the day before. The photos showed John and Yoko standing completely naked—one facing front and the other facing the back—and John himself had taken them with a time-delay camera in order to use them as the front and back covers for their album *Unfinished Music No. 1: Two Virgins* which featured the music that John and Yoko had created on their memorable first date four months previously. Apple Records released the album in December 1968, but in the face of public outrage, distributors decided to sell it in a plain brown wrapper that hid everything except for John's and Yoko's heads. Papered over or not, thousands of copies of the album were impounded as obscene in several jurisdictions; some thirty thousand copies were confiscated upon their arrival at New Jersey's Newark Airport, and in Chicago, the vice squad closed down a record shop for displaying the album's cover shorn of its wrapper.

When John returned to the living room with the cups of

tea, I told him that I'd been looking at the two photos on the wall, and asked if he wouldn't mind telling me something about them.

"I'm a ham photographer, you know," John said, "and I took the photos with me Nikon that I was kindly given by a commercially minded Japanese person when I was in Japan, along with me Pentax, me Canon, me boom-boom, and all the others. So I just set it up and took the photos with a delayed-action shutter right here in this flat."

"Bob Dylan," I pointed out to him, "once sang: 'But even the president of the United States / Sometimes must have to stand naked.' But how do you think people are going to react to the cover for your album?"

"Well, we've got that to come," he told me. "The thing is, I started with a pure . . . it was the *truth*, it was done with naïveté, and it was only after I'd got into it and done it and looked at it that I realized what kind of a scene I was going to create. Suddenly there it was, and suddenly you show it to people and then you know what the world's going to do to you, or try to do. But you have no knowledge of it when you conceive it or make it. Originally, I was going to record Yoko, and I thought the best picture of her for an album would be her naked. I was just going to record her as an artist. We were only on those kinds of terms then. So after that, when we got together, it just seemed natural for us, if we made an album together, for *both* of us to be naked. Of course, I've never seen me prick on an album or on a photo before: 'Whatnearth, there's a fellow with his prick out!' And that was the first I realized me prick was out, you know. I mean, you can see it on the photo itself, because we're naked in front of a camera, and that comes over in the eyes, so just for a minute you go"—and John made a face that looked a bit like Edvard Munch's *The Scream*—"I mean, you're not used to it, being naked."

"How do you face the fact that people are going to pillory you?" I asked.

"I know it won't be comfortable walking around with all the lorry drivers whistling and that, but it'll all die out. Next year it'll be nothing, like miniskirts or bare tits or whatever. It isn't anything. We're all naked really. When people attack Yoko and me, we know they're paranoiac. It's the ones that don't know, and you know they don't know—they're just going round in a blue fuzz. We don't worry too much. The thing is, the album also says: Look, lay off, will you? It's just two people—what have we done?"

"The comedian Lenny Bruce," I mentioned to him, "once compared himself to a doctor, saying that if people weren't sick—if they were healthy—there wouldn't be any need for him."

"That's the bit, isn't it?" John agreed. "Since the Beatles started being more natural in public—the four of us—we've really had a lot of knocking. I mean, we're always natural, we can't help it, we wouldn't be where we are if we hadn't been that way. We couldn't always think of what other people

83

were going to think all the time, otherwise we wouldn't have done anything. And we wouldn't have been us either. It took four of us to enable us to do what we've done—we couldn't have done it alone and kept that up."

"I've noticed, though, that people tend to be on your case more than the others," I pointed out.

"Yeh, I don't know why I get knocked more often," he said. "I seem to open me mouth more often. Something happens, and I forget what I am till it all happens again. I mean, we *all* get knocked—from the underground, the pop world—and me personally. They're all doing it. And now there are some *very* nasty remarks about Yoko being written. Just cruel. You just have to hold your breath and wait. They've got to stop soon."

"Couldn't you and Yoko just go off and create your own small community and not be bothered with all of this?" I wondered.

"Well, it's just the same there, you see. India was a taste of that—it's the same. So say there's a small community, but it's the same gig, it's all relative. There's no escape. There's no point in dropping out, because it's the same there and things have got to change. But I really think it all comes down to changing your head . . . and, sure, I know that's a cliché."

"Your recent *You Are Here* exhibition at the Robert Fraser Gallery gave critics another chance to take a swipe at you," I reminded him.

"Oh, right, but putting it on was taking a swipe at *them*

in a way. I mean, that's what it was about. A lot of them were saying, well, if it hadn't been John Lennon, nobody would have gone to it. Now, of course, if it had been Sam Bloggs, it would have been nice, but the point of it was that it was *me* doing it. And they're using that as a reason to say why it didn't work. Work as what?"

"This past summer, you and Yoko made a film called *Smile* which was taken with a high-speed camera and which shows your face in close-up smiling for fifty-one minutes in super-slow motion. Do you think this film would have worked as well if it had been just anyone smiling?"

"Yeh," he said, "it would work with somebody else smiling, but Yoko went through all this. It originally started out that she wanted a million people all over the world to send in a snapshot of themselves smiling, and then it got down to lots of people smiling, and then maybe one or two . . . and then *me* smiling as a symbol of today smiling—and that's what I am, whatever that means. And that's going to be the hang-up, of course, because it's me again. But they've got to see it someday—it's only me. I don't mind if people go to the film to see me smiling because it doesn't matter, it's not harmful. The idea of the film won't really be dug for another fifty or a hundred years probably. That's what it's all about. I just happen to be that face."

"I've only seen you and Yoko for a couple of days," I remarked, "but I think it's a shame that people can't come down here individually to see how you're both living. If you don't mind my saying so, you really seem to be two unusually fascinating and creative individuals who really respect and like each other's work—as well as each other."

"Well, that's it," John acknowledged. "I didn't see Ringo and his wife Maureen for about a month when I first got together with Yoko, and there were rumors going around about the film and all that. Maureen was saying she really had some strange ideas about where we were at and what we were up to. And there were some strange reactions from all me friends and at Apple about Yoko and me and what we were doing—'Have they gone mad?' But of course it was just us, you know, and if *they* are puzzled or reacting strangely to us two being together and doing what we're doing, it's not hard to visualize the rest of the world really having some amazing image."

"Recently," I said, "you've been criticized by a few people on the left for not using your influence to encourage people to blow up the establishment. Even *Time* magazine came out and said, look, the Beatles in their song 'Revolution' are saying 'no' to destruction."

"If destruction's the only way that some people can do it," John remarked, "there's nothing I can say that could influence them, 'cause that's where they're at, really. We've *all* got that in us, too, and that's why I sang the 'out and in' bit on a few takes and also in the TV version of 'Revolution'—'But when you talk about destruction / Don't you know that you can count me out (in)'—like yin and yang. I prefer 'out,' but we've got the other bit in us too. I don't know what I'd be doing if I was in their position. I don't think I'd be so meek and mild. I just don't know."

Just then, Yoko came into the living room and told John that it was time to go to the recording session. John got up and went over to a closet, took out a blue denim jacket, put it on, and then the three of us walked to the front door. Outside, a car was waiting to drive them to Abbey Road Studios. We all shook hands, I thanked them for the great two days, and they got into the car. Once inside, John rolled down one of the windows, and I quickly remarked to him how nice it would be if his smile could somehow become contagious. "The whole world really could use a little sympathetic magic," I told him.

"Yeh, a happy man can make a room happy, don't you think?" he replied . . . with a smile. "Yoko and I think that if everyone is sending out happiness to a degree here and there—or non-violent or non-hateful vibrations—they're bound to counteract some of the hate, even if you're doing it in a room like a yogi. And I believe you can. Goodbye for now," he waved, "and see you soon."

Speaking about the Beatles, John once told me, "When the four of us make it, we're one, but when we don't, we're one person in turmoil." In 1962, John, Paul,

George, and Ringo had taken up arms like musical muske-teers—"one for all and all for one." But now, six years later, as they began working on their *White Album*, the group's tempers and musical seams were visibly fraying, and their motto, for all intents and purposes, had mutated into "one for one and none for all." As John would later tell Jann Wenner: "Listen—all you experts listen, none of you can hear. Every track on that album is an individual track—there isn't any Beatle music on it. It was John and the Band, Paul and the Band, George and the Band. It was just me and a back-ing group, Paul and a backing group"—though a song like "Birthday" was certainly an exception to that rule. And as he later declared to David Sheff: "You know the song 'Wedding Bells Are Breaking Up That Old Gang of Mine'? The old gang of mine was over the moment I met Yoko. I didn't con-sciously know it at the time, but that's what was going on. As soon as I met her, that was the end of the boys, but it so happened that the boys were well known and weren't just the local guys at the bar."

Throughout the *White Album* recording sessions, John insisted that Yoko sit constantly by his side, and the other three Beatles felt it a thorn in theirs. "You know," Yoko told me when I spoke to her in her Dakota office, "when I first met the Beatles, John and I were so involved with each other that we couldn't see straight almost, we were really in a daze, really in a dream, just looking at each other, and we couldn't see anyone around us. And we didn't have the space to even consider what we looked like to other people—we were in our own world. And I realize now that we were closing everybody out. But even through that kind of strange mind, I really saw each of the Beatles as a very sensitive and brilliant artist."

"It's no secret," I remarked to her, "that you were maligned and scapegoated by many Beatles fans for supposedly causing the group to break up."

"I think that each of the Beatles was too strong and tough an individual to have been influenced by me in any way," she responded. "That's insanity to say that. Three very strong men don't listen to anybody, and these were three very talented people who really had too many songs for just one group. And I knew that each one of them was going to blossom out on his own. When I went to those recording sessions I immediately realized that it was sort of like having Mozart and Beethoven and Schubert in one group. I mean, Bob Dylan was doing everything alone, and the Beatles were doing it as four people—it's unusual that four guys should always be together, it was very tough, and then in comes a fifth person . . . and it was too much."

It even was too much for the drummer. One day at the end of August during the *White Album* recording sessions, Ringo decided that he'd, as he said, "had it." As he explained the situation: "I felt that the other three were really happy and I was an outsider. I went to see John . . . and I said, 'I'm leaving the group because I'm not playing well and I feel unloved and out of it, and you three are really close.' And John said, 'I thought it was *you* three!' So then I went over to Paul's and knocked on his door. I said the same thing: 'I'm leaving the band. I feel you three guys are really close and I'm out of it.' And Paul said, 'I thought it was *you* three!' I didn't even bother going to George then. I said, 'I'm going on holiday.' I took the kids and we went to Sardinia."

Ringo spent two weeks on the actor Peter Sellers's yacht, and one day, after the captain—to Ringo's dismay—served him squid and chips instead of cod and chips, the captain began expounding on the subject of octopuses. "He told me," Ringo said, "that they hang out in their caves and they go around the seabed finding shiny stones and tin-can bottles to put in front of their caves like a garden. I thought this was fabulous because at the time I just wanted to be under the sea too. A couple of tokes later with the guitar—and we had 'Octopus's Garden'!" ("We would be so happy you and me . . . In an octopus's garden with you.")

Shortly after writing what George Harrison once described as this "peaceful" and "cosmic" song—only the second one the drummer had ever written—Ringo received an importuning telegram from his "ex"-bandmates that read: "You're the best rock 'n' roll drummer in the world. Come on home. We love you." And when Ringo returned to Abbey Road Studios, he found his drum kit decked out with enough flowers to have sent Ferdinand the Bull into a state of permanent bliss.

On October 13, 1968, John sat alone with his acoustic guitar at the Abbey Road Studios and recorded "Julia," the thirtieth and final song of the *White Album*—a reverie from the etheric realm in which a son introduces to his departed mother the lover who is displacing her, though the images of both mother and lover are interlaced in his memory. It was his first-ever solo track—half sung, half spoken—and one of the most haunting songs he would ever write ("When I cannot sing my heart / I can only speak my mind").

"Yoko and I lived together for a year before we got married," John once remarked, "but we were still tied to other people by a bit of paper. One day some guy came in and said, here's your divorce papers, you're free—and the release was like a burden we didn't know we were carrying." So on March 20, 1969, he and Yoko flew by private plane to Gibraltar—because, as John said, it was "quiet, British, and friendly"—where they were granted an instant marriage license and joined in matrimony by the registrar at the British consulate. The bride wore a white minidress, a wide-brimmed white hat, and white socks; the groom was dressed in a white suit. Both were shod in white tennis shoes. A month later in London, John would stand in front of a Commissioner for Oaths and officially discard his middle name, "Winston," and assume the name "John Ono Lennon." "Yoko changed her name for me," he said, "and I've changed mine for her. One for both, both for each other."

In his novel *Wind, Sand and Stars*, Antoine de Saint-

Exupéry wrote: "Love does not consist in looking at each other, but in looking together in the same direction." In their first hours, days, and months together, John and Yoko had eyes only for each other—all for love and the world well lost. But five days after getting married, they turned their eyes in the direction of the Netherlands, having decided to publicly celebrate their honeymoon by engaging in a Bed-In for Peace in the Presidential Suite of the Amsterdam Hilton. When a journalist inquired why they had thought up such a harebrained scheme, John replied: "We're staying in bed for a week to register our protest against all the suffering and violence in the world. Can you think of a better way to spend seven days? It's the best idea we've had yet." Through their Apple office in London, John and Yoko sent me and a couple of other journalists a message suggesting that we join them for the postnuptial celebration. "When was the last time you were invited to a honeymoon? It may not happen again, you know." But work was going to keep me in London, and in any case, I knew that they wouldn't be at a loss for company.

It is hardly surprising that both John and Yoko were so passionate and unremitting in their commitment to the cause of peace. Yoko had been a war child—I would later learn that she had survived the firebombing of Tokyo at the end of World War II—and John a war baby, born on October 9, 1940, during a lull in the Luftwaffe's Liverpool blitz. War was imprinted on their earliest memories and innermost beings, so it was not surprising that all they were say-

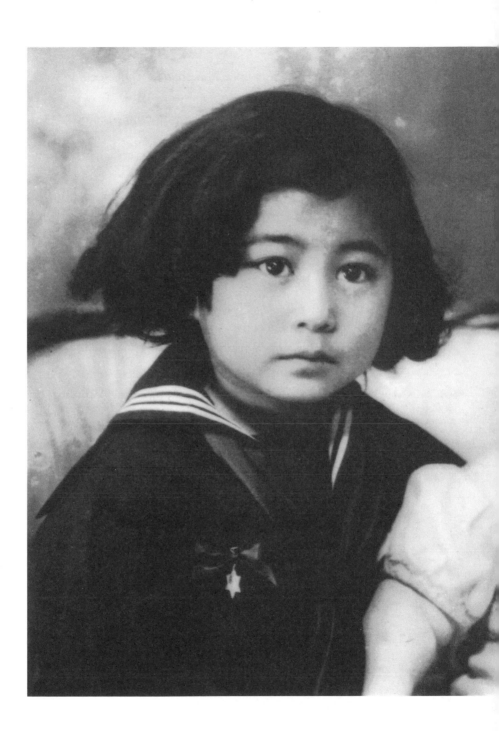

ing was give peace a chance and that all they seemed to be doing was, as John once sang, "chanting the mantra peace on earth." "Day after day, night after night," John reminded me when I spoke to him years later, "all over the TV there were Vietnamese dripping blood, and the newspapers were filled with headlines of horror. But you couldn't just sit around *wanting* it to go away, so Yoko and I decided to get some peace in the headlines for a change."

With their Bed-In—a work of performance art specifically inspired by Yoko's instruction pieces—John and Yoko practiced what they preached. "We're selling peace at whatever the cost," John declared to journalists at the time. "Yoko and I are just one big advertising campaign. . . . We are all Christ and we are all Hitler. We want Christ to win. We're trying to make Christ's message contemporary. What would he have done if he had advertisements, records, films, TV, and newspapers? Christ made miracles to tell his message. Well, the miracle today is communications, so let's use it."

Clad in pajamas and white bathrobes, propped up on their pillows, and surrounded by hand-painted signs reading "Hair Peace," "Bed Peace," "I Love Yoko," and "I Love John," they talked for a week, from 9 a.m. to 9 p.m., to some two hundred members of the world press who had undertaken the pilgrimage to their bedside—an occasion that John celebrated in his song "The Ballad of John and Yoko": "The newspaper said, 'Say, what you doing in bed?' / I said, 'We're only trying to get us some peace.' " As he later

remarked, "You should have seen the faces on the reporters and the cameramen fighting their way through the door! Because whatever it is, is in people's minds—and their minds were full of what they thought was going to happen. They fought their way in, and their faces dropped. There we were like two angels in bed, with flowers all around us, and peace and love in our heads." In fact, a John and Yoko Bed-In was nothing less than a Human Be-In that took place in a hotel bedroom rather than in a park, transforming it into a Community of Love and an Abode of Peace. (The Amsterdam Hilton now offers the John and Yoko Honeymoon Suite for about $2,000 a night, and allows couples to be married there in a civil ceremony.)

Two months later, on May 26, John and Yoko flew to Montreal in order to get some more peace, and staged their second weeklong Bed-In at the Queen Elizabeth Hotel, talking to visiting journalists and giving telephone interviews to radio stations in the United States and Canada. Montreal newspapers covering the event displayed headlines like MARRIED COUPLE ARE IN BED and THEY ARE GETTING UP TODAY. On the Bed-In's final weekend, John and Yoko rented four microphones and a four-track tape recorder from a local recording studio and enlisted a potpourri of inspirited visitors like Timothy Leary, Rabbi Abraham L. Feinberg, Tommy Smothers, Allen Ginsberg, Petula Clark, Dick Gregory, members of the Canadian chapter of the Radha Krishna Temple, along with every reporter in the room, to join them in singing the chorus of John's "Give Peace a Chance." Visitors banging on doors and tabletops, along with several Hare Krishna drummers, provided the trance-inducing rhythm section. John originally credited Paul McCartney as the co-writer of the song, but it was, in fact, John's first independent single.

Six months later, on November 15, Pete Seeger led half a million demonstrators in singing this anthem—the *Dona Nobis Pacem* of our time—at the Washington Monument where they had gathered to protest the Vietnam War. It was the largest single antiwar protest in U.S. history, whose participants John might well have been describing in his song "Mind Games"—millions of soul-powered "mind guerrillas" radiating the message of peace and love. And when John later saw television footage of the event, he declared it to be "one of the biggest moments of my life."

"After we finished doing interviews and talking to people and everyone else had gone away," Yoko recalled to the biographer Philip Norman, "it was the nicest time in our lives. One night, there was a beautiful full moon in the sky and no clouds, and John said, 'Well, we're going to keep on writing songs together, and our songs are going to be played all over the world. That's our life. That's how it's going to be.' It was just the moon and us. It was great."

All of John and Yoko's peace events were undertaken, as he explained, "in the tradition of Gandhi, only with a sense of humor." Regarding his two Bed-Ins for Peace, London's

Daily Mirror commented: "A not inconsiderable talent seems to have gone completely off his rocker"; but John proudly compared Yoko and himself to Laurel and Hardy. The *Daily Mirror* took him at his word and in 1969 crowned him Clown of the Year. Upon receiving news of this accolade, John responded: "In Paris, the Vietnam peace talks have got about as far as sorting out the shape of the table they're going to sit round. Those talks have been going on for months. In one week in bed, we achieved a lot more . . . A little old lady from Wigan or Hull wrote to the *Daily Mirror* asking if they could put Yoko and myself on the front page more often. She said she hadn't laughed so much for ages. That's great! . . . I wouldn't mind dying as the world's clown. I'm not looking for epitaphs." John certainly would have had the last laugh if he had known that in 1994, the self-proclaimed Republic of Abkhazia would issue two postage stamps featuring the faces of John and Groucho Marx, rather than portraits of Vladimir Lenin and Karl Marx, in order to spoof Abkhazia's Soviet past.

"We're all sharing the world together," John once declared. He and Yoko unceasingly proclaimed that their lives were their art, and their art their lives; that there was no line between what was private and public; and that, finally, there was nothing to hide—as John titled one of his songs, "Everybody's Got Something to Hide Except Me and My Monkey." "What's the big secret?" he once asked. "The secret," he said, "is there is no secret."

O n the Beatles' *White Album*, John wearily sang: "I'm so tired, I haven't slept a wink / I'm so tired, my mind is on the blink." And on *Rubber Soul*, Paul McCartney sang: "I'm looking through you / you're not the same." After almost ten years of being inseparable members of the Fab Four collective each of the Beatles had now begun to accept the fact that the dream was over. As George Harrison confessed, "Everybody had tried to leave, so it was nothing new. Everybody was leaving for years"; and as John told the television talk-show host Dick Cavett in 1971, "It's just that you grow up. We don't want to be the Crazy Gang or the Marx Brothers where you're being dragged onstage playing 'She Loves You' when we've got asthma and tuberculosis when we're fifty. You know, [*singing*] 'Yesterday, all my troubles seemed so far away.'"

On the morning of January 30, 1969, I received a phone call from the Beatles' press officer, Derek Taylor, who suggested that I might be pleasantly surprised if I immediately made my way over to the Apple Corps headquarters at 3 Savile Road. When I arrived there, I noticed a large crowd of office workers and midday shoppers milling around the street with their perplexed faces raised heavenward, attempting to identify the source of the familiar sounds of an amplified rock band. Up on the roof, the Beatles were playing their last live concert together, and members of the crowd were already offering their opinions. "Bloody stupid place to have a concert. It just is," griped one man. "You can't beat them. Style of their own. Lovely crowd," a woman disagreed. "Jolly good," another woman concurred, adding: "And nice to have something for free in this country!"

Since January 2, the group had spent more than one hundred hours being filmed for a cinema-verité–style documentary by director Michael Lindsay-Hogg, mainly on the large soundstage at the Twickenham Sound Studios, as they rapped, kibitzed, joked, griped, and bickered while rehearsing songs for their *Let It Be* album, which was first released in 1970 as part of a box set entitled *The Beatles Get Back*. Included in that box set—now a collector's item—was a 164-page glossy paperback book, the first and only one ever commissioned by the Beatles. Conceived of and produced by Neil Aspinall, the head of Apple Corps, it contained hundreds of now-iconic photographs taken by Ethan Russell, who had also taken the photos that accompanied my first *Rolling Stone* interview with John, as well as a text that included commentary about and dialogue from the Beatles' rehearsals. As one of the co-authors (along with writer David Dalton), I watched more than twenty hours of film footage and listened to an equal number of audio tapes of the Beatles at work, thus becoming inescapably familiar with the strained group dynamics at play at those *Let It Be* rehearsals.

During one of the sessions, for example, Paul reminded John and George that since the death of their manager Brian Epstein they had become disengaged from their music and each other. "That's why all of us have been sick of the group, you know," Paul admonished them one day. "The only way for it not to be a drag is for the four of us to think: Should we make it positive or should we forget it? It's like everything you do, you always need discipline. We've never had discipline. Mr. Epstein, he said, 'Get your suits on' and we did. It's like when you're growing up and then your daddy goes away, and then you have to stand on your own feet. Daddy has gone away now, you know, and we're on our own little holiday camp. I think we either go home or we do it." And as Paul took on the role of "Daddy"—at one point he turned to John and said, "Now look, son"—so George played "Bad Boy," telling Paul, "Well, if that's what doing it is, I don't want to do anything."

But there were also lighthearted, jabberwocky-mocking moments, as when John and Ringo began playing ventriloquist and dummy with each other:

JOHN: Bognor Regis is a tartan that covers Yorkshire.
    Rutland is the smallest county. Scarborough is a college
    scarf. And still the boon wasn't over, the Queen of Sheba
    wore falsies.
RINGO: I didn't know that.
JOHN: Didn't you know that? You weren't there at the time.
    Cleopatra was a carpet manufacturer.
RINGO: I didn't know that.
JOHN: John Lennon . . .

RINGO: A patriot!

JOHN: I didn't know that.

And there were also some occasional enraptured moments and romantic interludes, as when, on the darkened soundstage, John and Yoko waltzed together across the studio floor like mercurial shadows, while George hauntingly sang "All through the night / I, me, mine, I, me, mine, I, me, mine."

To provide a conclusion to the film, the Beatles had agreed to give one last public concert, which, at various times, they fantasized might take place at a Tunisian amphitheater, an Egyptian pyramid, the Liverpool Cathedral, the Houses of Parliament, or possibly on an ocean liner, "singing the middle eight as the sun comes up." With only a few days left to decide, John told the others: "Just suggest where: Pakistan, the moon—I'll still be there till you don't let me down. You'll be surprised at the story that will come out of this." And then, in a final moment of desperation, John had a flash of inspiration: "I'm warming to the idea of doing it in an asylum."

By default, they finally decided to perform an impromptu concert "up on the roof" of the five-story Apple Corps building, as if they were taking their cue from the words of the classic Gerry Goffin–Carole King song of the same name in which the singer, who's finding the world too much to face, climbs to the top of the stairs and onto the roof where all his cares "just drift right into space." But the concert almost didn't take place. "About ten minutes before we were due to start," Lindsay-Hogg recalled, "all the Beatles were in a little room at the top of the stairs, and it still wasn't certain that they'd go ahead. George didn't want to and Ringo started saying he didn't really see the point. Then John said, 'Oh fuck—let's do it.' "

It was a cold and blustery afternoon, and on the windswept roof, it seemed as if the Beatles were actually performing on the upper deck of a ship. Paul wore a black dinner jacket, George was cloaked in a shaggy dark overcoat, Ringo sported an orange plastic mac, John had on Yoko's thick brown fur coat—and Billy Preston, who was playing keyboards with the group, was dressed in a brown leather jacket as he hunched over his electric piano. From the street below, I listened rapturously to the forty-two-minute concert that, in spite of all the acrimonious rehearsal foreplay, resounded with impassioned performances of songs like "I've Got a Feeling," "Don't Let Me Down," "Dig a Pony," as well as a heart- and time-stopping rendition of "One After 909," which John and Paul—looking once again like brothers-in-arms—had composed twelve years before when they were just teenagers besotted with Chuck Berry and Buddy Holly. As the Beatles began a second take of "Get Back," a contingent of blue-helmeted London bobbies, responding to complaints from incensed businessmen in nearby office buildings, made their way up the stairs and terminated the concert. And as Paul and George unstrapped their guitars, John stepped forward, faced the film crew, and said, "I'd like to say thank you on behalf of the group and ourselves, and I hope we passed the audition." It was the last time the Beatles would ever perform together in public.

On September 20, 1969, John, Paul, George, and Ringo, along with their manager, Allen Klein, gathered for a business meeting in Apple's boardroom to discuss the group's future plans. At its conclusion, like a bolt from the blue, John fired the verbal shot that would shortly be heard round the world, and announced that he was leaving the group. "I started the band. I disbanded it—it's as simple as that," he said. (The other Beatles did not publicly confirm the break-up, however, until December 31, 1970, when Paul filed a lawsuit in order to dissolve the group.) John had everything he needed, he was an artist, and he didn't plan to look back. "Afterwards, John and I went off in the car," Yoko recalled to Philip Norman, "and he turned to me and said, 'That's it with the Beatles. From now on, it's just you—okay?'" Henceforth, life for John would be lived in the spirit of the American country singer Jimmie Rodgers's song "You and My Old Guitar": "In a one horse town or city, no matter where we are / I'm happy if I have with me you and my old guitar."

The English author Samuel Johnson famously said that when a man was tired of London, he was tired of life. But John was just waking up, a new life was beckoning, and it was gradually enticing both him and Yoko overseas to the Empire City. He often spoke of his having "graduated" from Liverpool to London, and from London to New York, and even compared the Brooklyn accent to Liverpudlian Scouse. "I should have been born in New York," he declared to Jann Wenner. "I should have been born in Greenwich Village—that's where I belong. Why wasn't I born there? Paris was it in the eighteenth century. London, I don't think, has ever been it, except literary-wise, when Wilde and Shaw and all of them were there. Everybody heads toward the center." And Yoko once reported that "even when John was in Liverpool and London, he used to show me that famous Bob Dylan album cover, where Dylan's walking with that girl [Suze Rotolo on the cover of *The Freewheelin' Bob Dylan*], and John would say, 'That should have been me, I could have been a New Yorker!' "

Because of John's previous marijuana conviction in a British court in 1968, John and Yoko were granted only B-2 "temporary visitor for pleasure" visas to the United States that were scheduled to expire in February 1972—Yoko had never been granted U.S. citizenship, and her previously issued green card had lapsed—and before they took up residence in Greenwich Village in November 1971, they were frequent but only part-time visitors to New York City.

In December 1970, John and Yoko arrived in the city for their first time as a couple; Yoko, who had lived there on and off between 1956 and 1966, hadn't been back in four years. "As far as I was concerned," John remarked, "it was just like returning to your wife's hometown." When he had previously visited New York as a Beatle, he had been able to see the city only through the windows of limousines, so Yoko now showed him New York through her eyes—taking him for walks in Central Park and along the Hudson River, exploring the pre-gentrified East Village, and showing him some of her old haunts. "Yoko made me walk around the streets and parks and squares and examine every nook and cranny," John said. "In fact, you could say I fell in love with New York on a street corner." They visited some of Yoko's old downtown-artist friends, and sneaked out on their own for afternoon screenings of movies—something John had never been able to do in London—such as *Diary of a Mad Housewife* and *Lovers and Other Strangers*. They even made two new films of their own for inclusion in a three-evening John and Yoko mini–film festival at the Elgin Theater.

I myself had moved back from London to my hometown of New York in early 1970 and continued to work for *Rolling Stone* as an associate editor. On December 2, I received a phone call from Yoko who asked me if I would like to appear in one of the films that she and John were co-directing. "It's called *Up Your Legs Forever*," she informed me. "What role will I be playing?" I asked her. She explained that she and John were recruiting more than three hundred people to take off all of their clothes, except for their underwear, and donate their legs for peace. "We can't have peace," she stated, "until we expose ourselves to each other. After you communicate like that, then maybe we can have peace. And everyone who's in the film, including *you*," she assured me, "will be a star."

So on the afternoon of December 4, I made my way to a soundstage on West Sixty-first Street, along with artists such as Larry Rivers, George Segal, and Peter Max; the writer Tom Wolfe; the Beatles' manager, Allen Klein; New York filmmakers D. A. Pennebaker, Shirley Clarke, Jack Smith, and Jonas Mekas; several society notables; and underground personalities like Paul Krassner, Taylor Mead, and David Johansen. We all stripped off our clothes and stood on a podium, one at a time and one after another, as a movie camera panned up our bare legs from our toes to our upper thighs. In recompense for our toil, every volunteer received a one-dollar bill, as well as a black-and-white photo that John had taken of each of us with his Instamatic camera. I spent the dollar, but I still keep that photo—which embarrassingly shows me standing on the podium with arms akimbo, a scarf around my neck, and wearing only my briefs—under lock and key. "When people look at the legs," Yoko remarked to me after the shoot, "they'll see that there's no difference between famous and not-so-famous legs, intellectual and non-intellectual legs. When it comes to legs, titles or fame or power or money are of no importance because we're all just very modest beings. We all have pretty ordinary legs—men and women, old and young." "But just *human* legs!" I observed. "Yes," Yoko said, laughing. "Just human legs . . . and human legs are very peaceful!"

Up Your Legs Forever was an insouciant divertissement. But on December 11—just one week after the film's completion—John and Yoko simultaneously released their two debut solo albums. Entitled *John Lennon/Plastic Ono Band* and *Yoko Ono/Plastic Ono Band*, these companionate recordings—the two halves of one musical sky—shared matching album-cover photos that showed John and Yoko, as if in a waking dream, lying under a tree in an English garden suffused with pale green light. On Yoko's album cover, she is reclining on John's lap; on John's, he is reclining on hers. By contrast, the black-and-white photograph on the cover of John and Yoko's first musical collaboration, *Unfinished Music No. 1: Two Virgins*, depicted them standing next to each other completely naked. On their two new albums, however, John and Yoko shed all of their emotional garments and exposed their hearts in songs that Yoko described as "stark-naked real" and that, again in Emily Dickinson's words, really did make you feel as if the top of your head were taken off.

In early March 1970, nine months before moving to New York, John had received a package in the mail containing a book by California psychotherapist Arthur Janov, which was being sent to celebrities in order to solicit endorsements. John opened the package, glanced at the book's title—*The Primal Scream*—then read a few pages. "John passed the book over to me," Yoko recalled, "and he said to me, 'Look . . . it's you.' " It was also, of course, John himself, and as he confessed, "Something about it rang a lot of bells."

The book described a novel therapeutic technique that Janov called Primal Therapy, which involved a patient reexperiencing repressed childhood pain and traumas through emotional and cathartic outbursts called "primals." John immediately telephoned Janov at his Los Angeles home and convinced him to come to England to work with him and Yoko. The psychologist flew over to see them for three weeks, and spent time talking to John about his motherless and fatherless early childhood. "He was just one big ball of pain," Janov later remarked. "This was someone the whole world adored, and it didn't change a thing. At the center of all that fame and wealth and adulation was just a lonely little kid." John would later say that, like most people, his ability to feel had been switched off, and that Primal Therapy had provided him with the means to switch back into being a baby and to reexperience the world like a child. "The thing in a nutshell," John declared, "is that Primal Therapy allowed us to feel feeling continually, and those feelings usually make you cry. That's all."

Janov suggested that John and Yoko continue their treatments at his Primal Center in Los Angeles. So in late May,

John and Yoko flew to California where for four months they engaged in one-on-one sessions with Janov and participated in group sessions with the other patients. The German poet Novalis posited the fascinating notion that "every disease is a musical problem, every cure a musical solution." While undergoing therapy at the center, John and Yoko were moved to start writing some new songs, and after returning to London in September, they spent four weeks at Abbey Road Studios recording them with Klaus Voormann on bass, Ringo on drums, and John on guitars and piano.

In his song "Just Like a Woman," Bob Dylan had sung: "Nobody feels any pain." But on his explosive new album, John unflinchingly resolved to feel it, and envisioned a way to strip down words and music to their essence in order to do so. In the second-century once-secret Gospel of Thomas, Jesus declares: "If you bring forth what is within you, what you bring forth will save you. If you do not bring forth what is within you, what you do not bring forth will destroy you." And in the wake of his therapeutic breakthroughs, John brought forth from the shaken childhood heart within him songs like "Mother," "Isolation," and "God" ("The dream is over / What can I say?"). Upon the album's release, the critic Greil Marcus declared that "John's singing on the last verse of 'God' may be the finest in all of rock."

On *Yoko Ono/Plastic Ono Band*, Yoko brought forth her own cri de coeur, as she assembled and created shattering vocal compositions such as "Why," "Touch Me," and "Paper Shoes" from the free-form jam sessions recorded at the same time that John was making his record. "It was getting light outside when I finished making my album on the remix board," Yoko said, "and I felt like Madame Curie discovering a new sound world." Most John Lennon and Beatles fans responded to Yoko's album as if it were a land mine, but in a glowing review, the critic Dave Marsh described Yoko as "the first rock scat singer." And to the astonishment of many of Yoko's onetime detractors, *Yoko Ono/Plastic Ono Band* has proved to be an abiding influence on punk, new wave, no wave, noise rock, and electronica musicians throughout the world.

Ever since my first meeting with Yoko in London in 1968, I had always wanted to talk with her at length about her life and work. In November 1970, Jann Wenner suggested that I write an extended profile of her for *Rolling Stone,* and for that purpose, Yoko invited me to spend the evening with her and John on Sunday, December 13—two days following the release of *Yoko Ono/Plastic Ono Band*—at the Regency Hotel where they were staying over the Christmas holiday. When I entered their hotel suite, Yoko asked me if I wouldn't mind beginning our interview a little bit later because tonight the music from her new album was going to be featured on Alex Bennett's WMCA call-in radio program.

She led me into the bedroom where John was standing by the bedside table turning on the radio. I sat in a soft cushion chair, and John and Yoko relaxed on their bed as we began listening to the program. "Tonight is a really special night," Alex Bennett announced enthusiastically, "because we're going to be playing music by Yoko Ono from her first-ever solo album. It's not like anything you've ever heard before, and there are people who are going to love it and people who are going to hate it, but I think that in 1980 music will probably sound like this. So let's start right off with the song called 'Why.' Get ready to phone in and tell us what you think."

Suddenly the awakening thunderclap of a woman's voice and a fusillade of guitar shots shattered the radio airwaves like William Burroughs's "screaming glass blizzards of enemy flak," blindsiding listeners with driving dance-punk rhythms, piercing sonics, and the uncanny screams, wails, cries, moans, howls, and caterwauls of what sounded like a stricken, desperately hurting, and cruelly abandoned banshee child. So as not to interrupt this explosive music, John passed a notepad over to me on which he had written "It's today's 'Tutti Frutti'!"—the classic Little Richard song with its insurrectionary cry of "A-wop-bop-a-loo-bop-a-lop-bam-boom!"—for John, the highest compliment he could pay.

"It's truly disastrous," a beleaguered-sounding man with a nasal voice called in to say, "and it's really making me crazy."

"I'm forty-nine years old," another listener remarked, "forty-nine, and I dig it."

"I'm listening to this," a woman declared nervously, "and it's scaring me."

"Hey there," someone else volunteered, "it's just like Ornette [Coleman] and Albert Ayler and [John] Coltrane. Great!"

"Enough!" a listener shouted, then slammed down the phone.

"It's music, you idiot!" John exclaimed as he gestured to the radio. "Because it's not got *da-da-da*, there's nothing for him to hook onto."

"You don't mind hearing the program?" Yoko asked John.

"I *want* to," he said. "You see, with Yoko's and my new album we're both looking at the same thing from different sides of the table. Mine's literate, hers is revolutionary. She's got a sixteen-track voice!"

"You know, Yoko," I remarked, as John turned down the radio, "I've often observed that when people see a visual image that bothers them, they just tend to dismiss it—out of sight, out of mind. But with regard to your voice, some listeners really seem to feel uncontrollably threatened by it. Have you wondered why that might be true?"

"Yes, that's interesting," she said. "I think it's because I'm not trying to use a pretty voice, I'm not trying to refine what comes out."

"The song 'Why' that we just heard," I commented, "is

like an unending scream of pain. Like someone crying out, Why am I here?"

"And why are you hurting me?" Yoko added. "And why don't you love me? There's all that grief and mourning. And in 'Why,' I really wanted to let go."

"You know, I'm playing guitar on that track," John mentioned to me.

"And those shattering explosions of sounds really remind me of the free jazz energy of Ornette Coleman's and Albert Ayler's music," I commented.

"Right," John said, "but you can't do that on a three-minute single, especially with an expert technician like George [Harrison] sitting around."

"We were beginning to record our two albums at the same recording session," Yoko explained. "And John was making his album first, but we decided that if I got inspired I should just join in. I really like the idea of jamming and improvising and going somewhere that you don't really know instead of planning everything . . . just letting things be decided by the wind or whatever.

"At one point during the session, John started doing something very unusual with his guitar, like [*sings a high-pitched drone sound*], and then he began shouting *Yah-Yah*, and he inspired me so much that I just jumped in and started to scream . . . and John's guitar was going frantic, and I'd go *Ahnnh*, and he'd go *Ahnnh*, and it became a dialogue with each of us stimulating the other. And on 'Why,' Ringo, who was playing drums with us and wasn't usually turned on by my singing, actually did a lot of things that inspired me too, and I began following *him*. We really didn't know who was inspiring who."

"In 'Why,' you're only screaming out that one word," I noted, "but in some of the other new songs on your album I can't really make out if you're singing words or not. In 'Paper Shoes,' which sounds to me a little bit like a Navajo night chant, you don't seem to be singing any words."

"Yes I do," Yoko said. "Listen! [*crying out*] *Pa-pa-pa-pa pa-per shooooooooes*. Just like that."

"Yes she does," John confirmed. And then, suddenly and spontaneously, they both began wailing together in overlapping counterpoint:

Yoko: *Pa-pa-pa-pa-pa pa-per* . . .

John: *Pa-per pa-per pa-per-pa-per-pa-per* . . .

Yoko*: Shoo-ooo-ooo-ooo-ooo-ooo* . . .

John: *Shoo-shoo shoo-shoo shoo-shoo-shoo-shoo* . . .

Together: [*screaming*] SHOOOOOOOES!

"Fantastic!" I exclaimed. "That's a performance worth bootlegging!"

"Yes," Yoko said, laughing, "I've realized that John and I have a very mad streak. And we're similar in that sense, really. There's something about us that's saying, 'Fuck you, we couldn't care less,' and I go mad with my voice, and he does that too with his guitar. We're not academic, we're too mad to stay being intellectuals—although we have that side, too, but we can't hold on to it. We always go back to the madness."

"Why is it that you often break up your words when you sing them—like *pa-pa-pa pa-per*?"

"You know," Yoko confessed, "when I'm embarrassed I sometimes start to stutter a little bit."

"And when she's tired, she stutters too," John interjected.

"I hope you won't mind my interrupting," I said, "but your talking about stuttering brought me back to something that happened a couple of years ago when I was living in London. I was walking by Belsize Square one night, and I noticed a mother breast-feeding her baby under a streetlamp that was flickering on and off. And while I was looking at that baby, the flickering made me think of the sound *ma-ma-ma-ma-ma*, and the image of the flickering light and the baby breast-feeding suddenly gave me that idea that stutterers are persons who have a difficult time giving birth to words."

"That's what it is," John said.

"And sometimes when I'm trying to say something, I'll begin to stutter," Yoko said. "Most of us kill off our real emotions, and on top of them you have your smooth self. It's like the pompous guy in the film *Diary of a Mad Housewife* with his singsong voice—'And-*now*-you-must-eat-your-*lunch*-and-after-*that*...' Like that. There's that unreal tone. But when I want to say 'I'm sorry' in a song, I don't feel like saying [*in a singsong voice*] 'I'm *sorry*, mother,' but

119

rather as an emotion should be [*groaning, stuttering*] 'I'm *so-or-or-orrrry.*' A stutterer is someone who's feeling something very *genuine*, not repressing yourself and talking too smoothly. So in 'Paper Shoes,' I say: *Pa-pa-pa-pa-paper sh-sh-sh-sh-shooooooes!*

"The older you get, the more frustrated you feel. And it gets to a point where you don't have time to utter a lot of intellectual bullshit. If you were drowning in a river, you wouldn't say, 'I'd like to be helped because I have just a moment to live.' You'd say, 'Help!' And if you were even more desperate you'd scream out *Ayyyiiiieeee!*, or something like that. And the desperation of life is really life itself, the core of life, what's simply driving us forth. When you're really desperate, it's simply phony to use descriptive and decorative adjectives to express yourself."

"But I've noticed that you express the other side of this as well," I mentioned to Yoko. "Like your quiet, gentle little song 'Who Has Seen the Wind?' that's the B side of John's 'Instant Karma!' "

"But on that song," Yoko explained, "you can hear that the voice is wavering, there are shrills and cracks, it's not professional pop singing, and the background is going off a little. There was something of a lost little girl about it. Because I didn't want it to be too pretty. What I was aiming for was the effect you get in Alban Berg's opera *Wozzeck*, where the drunkard is singing *aahghgaagh* in a slightly crazed voice, a bit of a broken toy, a kind of quiet desperation. And in 'Who Has Seen the Wind?' I was thinking of that. Like a woman who looks very gentle and sedate but is going all crazy inside."

"You know, Van Gogh's paintings might please you," John observed, "but you know damn well what shit he went through to do it. The pain is in the painting, but there's still this pleasure and warmth and color in it."

"To judge by your overwhelmingly intense new album," I said to John, "you seem to have gone through a lot of Van Gogh–type pain yourself. I only half-jokingly think of it as your 'Howlin' Wolf' record. I've never heard your voice and words come so perilously close to the emotional edge as they do in 'God,' 'Mother,' 'I Found Out,' and 'Well Well Well.' "

"You know," John responded, "I was a much looser singer when I was younger. But then I became more uptight, more . . . well, whatever you become when you become a famous something-or-other. And then I was also more self-conscious singing with Paul and George. On 'Twist and Shout' I was letting it go a bit, and also at certain stage shows when I could no longer control it, and I'd go beyond meself and just go crazy. But now that I'm on my own and can do what I like and not restrict meself, I'm allowing meself to sing the way I did when I was younger. Just letting go. I was beginning to let go again on 'Cold Turkey'—that was Yoko's influence. She excited me and I wanted to use my voice more."

"That song 'Cold Turkey,' " I said, "is so excruciating in

the way it makes the listener experience the pain of heroin withdrawal that you really could have included it on your new album, don't you think?"

"But when I listen to it now," John replied, "it really sounds to me like shit. I feel that I hadn't really let go and that I was still sort of *performing*. But I finally broke through this time."

"Just like many other people," I told him, "I was astonished by the risks you took making this album."

"Well, thank you," John said. "I just brought out what was in me."

"I can't imagine what you could do as a follow-up."

"Maybe I'll relax on the next one," John replied, laughing. "Maybe I'll do 'I Want to Hold Your Hand' or 'Tutti Frutti' or 'Long Tall Sally' just to get me out of this one, otherwise I'll just be having *that* hanging over me. And maybe Yoko will do a Lennon-McCartney album. I'm not going to be boxed in. I *refuse* to be *boxed* in."

"Do you feel people boxing you in here in New York because of your fame?" I asked.

"It's getting great because people don't bother me here at all. There was a guy up at my manager's office to cut my hair, and he didn't know who I was. 'Are you in show business?' he asked me. And I said, 'Well, I sing a bit, you know.' It's beautiful."

"Do you sometimes mind *not* being recognized?" I wondered.

"I *love* it," John exclaimed. "I'd like to be invisibly famous. I want all that love that fame brings, but not the hang-ups. I was always doing a lot of media things before because I needed their love, like they needed mine. But we couldn't stop it, it was the end of the road, and there were no more drugs to take. I mean, what can you do? I didn't want to just waste away like that. So I had a breakdown, and Yoko and I went to Primal Therapy for four months. Arthur Janov gave us a mirror, and I had to look into my own soul. It was fantastic . . . You go to therapy, right, Jonathan?"

"For years!"

"A lot of talking, right?"

"Right."

"That's symptomatic," John asserted. "That's what Janov is against. Read his book, Jonathan. You'll have to take a bit of time out of your life, but I promise you that this will be the last time you'll ever have to go to therapy!"

"Do you still do Primal Therapy?" I asked.

"No, because I know the whole process, the process now happens *without* me thinking. And Yoko and I don't need anybody else, we don't do any more therapy."

"But don't you sometimes still feel that anxiety in your body—"

"Every morning!"

"And what do you do with it?"

"Just *feel* it! Janov taught us how to feel it. We cry. You do it. It's all right, it stops after two hours, you can't go on more than four hours, your body gets tired like a baby. Cry. It's all over. Really, read the book, Jonathan . . . I promise you."

"And you want to know how Janov came up with the idea for Primal Therapy?" Yoko asked me. "It's an amazing story. What happened was that in 1966, I went to London for the first time—though I hadn't met John yet—to take part in DIAS."

"What was that?" I asked.

"It was called the Destruction in Art Symposium," she explained. "A lot of artists and poets from around the world came and did performance events and happenings and readings all over London for three weeks." At a lecture she gave at the symposium, Yoko spoke about her notions regarding the unexpected poetic relations between creation and destruction, noting that Japanese monks burned their temples in order to prevent them from deteriorating, and sometimes took off their pants before they fought. At DIAS, she also presented a dozen of her pieces, among the most powerful being *Shadow Piece*, in which she traced the outlines of twenty participants on a long sheet of cloth laid over a strip of land bombed during World War II and still littered with debris—a resonating reference to the imprints of vaporized bodies left on the sidewalks of Hiroshima after the atomic bombing—and then folded up the sheet of cloth and took the shadows prisoner; and *Cut Piece*, in which Yoko sat motionless onstage, with her knees folded under her, and invited members of the audience to cut off pieces of her clothing with scissors until she was left nearly naked. "People went on cutting the parts they do not like of me," she wrote in her 1966 booklet *Autobiography*, "finally there was only the stone remained of me that was in me but they were still not satisfied and wanted to know what it's like in the stone."

Just then, the phone rang, and Yoko picked up the receiver. "It's for me, John. I'll go into the next room to talk and you can tell Jonathan about that guy in the baby diapers."

"This all took place during Yoko's first trip to London, before I met her," John explained to me. "She was the only woman there to perform her own events, and she's told me about some of the things she did there . . . like *Whisper Piece*, which is like the Telephone Game. Yoko gave a word to a member of the audience, who then passed it on until it went all the way up through the balcony. Then the last guy came up onstage to tell her the word . . . and Yoko said, 'Don't tell me.' And that was the end of the piece.

"But the way this all connects to Arthur Janov and Primal Therapy is that there was a guy at DIAS who did a piece in which he dressed up in baby diapers and went around screaming 'Mommy! Daddy!' while sucking on a baby bottle. Now, it happened that one of Janov's patients had actually seen that performance, and later, when he started taking therapy with Janov in L.A.—and this was before Janov had conceived of Primal Therapy—the patient started to describe that guy's performance to Janov. And when it came to his trying to say 'Mommy,' Janov realized that the patient couldn't say the word. So Janov told him, 'Don't describe it to me, just tell me how it sounded' . . . and suddenly, instead of the description, this primal scream came out. The patient was taken over by his own scream, his own pain. The guy had like an epileptic fit in Janov's office, and he screamed like a baby from right within himself. And after that, he apparently got completely calm, and when he did, he just kept on repeating, 'I made it. I made it.' And that's how the whole Primal Therapy started up."

Yoko had reentered the bedroom as John was finishing this story. And she returned to the bed and lay down next to him.

"I became stronger when I met John because he and I help each other," she told me. "It's very tough for a woman artist to stand alone and do things. You get really very lonely. I also felt very lonely and emotionally deprived as a child. And John was like that too. It was something about my parents being so strict with me, and I felt that they were sort of trying to shape me into some kind of live doll, and I had a guilt complex about being there . . . and I felt like I wanted to disappear."

"It sounds," I remarked, "like your *Hide-and-Seek Piece* that goes: 'Hide until everybody goes home. Hide until everybody forgets about you. Hide until everybody dies.'"

"Everybody wants to be invisible," John said, turning to Yoko. "You just express it."

"You think people want to be invisible?" I asked him.

"Well, if we take it as read that everyone is deprived of

126

the amount of love they need, then the next thing after that is to say, 'There must be something wrong with me. And if it's my fault, I better get off the earth.'"

"But there are kids who do get love from their parents," I demurred.

"I suppose so," John replied, "but I don't know any. They get as much as their parents can give, but how much can their parents give? I've never met anyone who seems to have been satisfied."

"But some people," I argued, "are resilient enough to be loving regardless of what love or lack of love they got, don't you think?"

"I don't know. There probably are a few ... But don't worry about my backchat," John apologized. "Just carry on!"

"There comes a point," Yoko continued, "when you just can't keep on feeling 'I'm sorry I'm alive, I'm sorry I exist.' And I'm finally just beginning to think maybe I can live somehow, that I don't need to disappear anymore. So I've decided that I'm just going to *say* it, just break through and *say* it."

"It's just like being born," John added. "When you're born you scream, and when you want something you scream."

"In your new album," I said to Yoko, "it seems to me that you've now disappeared into *yourself* rather than just into the wind. Your voice is so intensely *there* that I feel that you've now entered into your real being. But maybe it's a bit pretentious to put it like that."

"No," Yoko said, "that's a nice way of saying it."

"And it's not pretentious," John interjected, "it's just that you have to express it in words. None of us are particularly articulate. But what you're actually saying is *right*. She *becomes* her voice, and you get touched!"

"I remember when I first met you in London in 1968," I told Yoko. "So many people were being so dismissive of you and your work that it kind of forced you to have to continually justify yourself all the time by making statements that sounded to other people as if you were trying too hard to prove a point. So you were trapped in a real double bind."

"Do you think so?" Yoko wondered.

"That's what I feel," I said, "but maybe I'm wrong."

"He's very insecure," John broke in and pointed at me. "I hope you don't mind, and this is just my observation, Jonathan, but you're just like her, I think. Whenever you make a correct statement, you immediately say, 'Well, I could be wrong.' And I think that I do that too."

"But it actually might be presumptuous of me—"

"No, you're *all right*," John responded. "It's like when you say to your parents, 'I'm hungry. Is that all right? I could be wrong but I'm hungry!' "

"But sometimes you feel that you've got to show that you're grateful," I said.

"Oh, that's it exactly," Yoko agreed.

"But whenever you're *right*, you say you could be *wrong*," John insisted. "And when you're not bothered, you don't mention it."

"You're just being apologetic," Yoko said to me in a comforting tone.

"It's just *guilt*," John asserted. "Yoko and I are like that too. We're all like that. The *world's* like that!"

John now got up and turned on the hotel television, then returned to the bed and, while half watching the soundless television screen, began reading an essay called "Concept Art" by Henry Flynt—a term that Flynt had first coined. One of Yoko's oldest friends from her avant-garde days in the early 1960s, Flynt was not only a writer of dense philosophical essays but also a composer and violinist who attempted to fuse avant-garde noise music with free jazz and Southern roots music, and unbeknownst to Yoko, he was also a rabid fan of songs like "Be-Bop-A-Lula," "Johnny B Goode," and "Willie and the Hand Jive." John and Yoko had recently visited him in his downtown New York City apartment.

"We went down to see him because we wanted to surprise him," John would later recount to me, "and we were told that you needed to know the secret knock in order to get into his flat. So we go to the door and do the secret knock—*boom de-de boom-boom*—and this guy comes out, and he's got no glasses on, so he's squinting and shouting, 'Who is it? Who is it?' And like he's wearing *Bermuda shorts*, and he takes us into this strange little room and puts on this record of him playing the violin. There was one track which was like *uhn-uhn-uhn-uhn-uhn*—just like that—and then another one with country stuff over what he said were *deeply complicated rhythms* . . . but it was fantastic!"

While John was lying in bed reading Flynt's essay, Yoko began to speak to me about *Bottoms*, her eighty-minute film that presents close-up shots of the naked, gently undulating buttocks of 365 of Yoko's friends as they walked on a treadmill—John once called the film *Many Happy Endings*—and it had created a small scandal when it was first shown in 1966. "Before I met John," Yoko told me, "I had become sort of famous because of *Bottoms*, but that was actually the loneliest time in my life. Some of the people in my avant-garde circle resented me because of my fame—at least in *that* circle!—and that made me feel isolated. But it was just empty fame. Now, when my record is played on the radio, I've got someone who's *happy* about it."

"You weren't really a rock 'n' roller in those days, were you?" I said to her kiddingly.

"Exactly. When I first went to the Beatles recording sessions I was just listening. And after one of the sessions I asked John, 'Why don't you use different rhythms instead of just going *ba-ba-ba-ba*?' And I realize now that it was really a kind of avant-garde snobbery on my part, because my voice was going *ugghhh . . . ghuhhhh*, but there was no beat. So I thought to myself [*simpering tone*] 'Well, simple music!'

"You see, I had been doing my Music of the Mind—no sound at all, everybody sitting around just imagining sounds. At my earlier New York City concerts I was throwing peas from a bag at people, and I had long hair and I was circling my hair and the movement was a sound. Even then, some people were saying that even *that* was maybe too theatrical, too animalistic. And then there was my *Wall Piece*, which instructed you to hit the wall with your head, and that was called too dramatic and too painful to watch as well . . . By the way, Jonathan, did you come to any of those concerts?"

"I'm really sorry I didn't," I told her, "but I was still a teenager in those days and had my head in the sand."

"That's amazing," Yoko said as she turned to John. "I'm talking to him like he's my generation, and he was a *kid* then!"

"Well, you were just born before me," I said apologetically.

"Yeh, it's all your fault!" John exclaimed, laughing.

"Whose fault?" I asked.

"Anyone's," he replied. "It's all our faults all the time!"

"Speaking of the Music of the Mind that you were doing in those days, Yoko," I continued, "I once read a wonderful story about a fourth-century Chinese poet who used to carry around a zither that didn't have any strings on it and on which he played mute music. And when people asked him to explain why he did this, he'd say, 'I only seek the meaning that lies at the heart of the zither. Why strain myself to produce sounds on the strings?' "

"Yes," Yoko responded, "intellectually I still think that

Music of the Mind is pretty far-out. But even then I was beginning to feel stifled with that, it was driving me crazy. I was dying to scream, to go back to my voice. I wanted to put some flesh and blood into it. John Cage and Morton Feldman were composing things that were very *cool*—it was a very *cool* art atmosphere in New York at that time. And I came to a point where I believed that the idea of avant-garde purity was just as stifling as just doing a rock beat over and over. There's just so much you can repeat. I probably could have kept on doing what I'd been doing all the time, but then it only becomes a stereotyped thing."

"But do you think you'll ever get back to doing the kind of performance pieces and happenings that you used to?" I asked her.

"Excuse me," John interrupted, as he put aside the Henry Flynt essay for a moment. "The Bed-Ins for Peace that we did in Amsterdam and Montreal last year were *direct* developments of what Yoko had been doing before . . . and those were *big* events. Also don't forget our WAR IS OVER! billboards and posters that we put up in twelve cities around the world. *That* was an event all right! . . . I didn't mean to interrupt, but I just overheard what Jonathan was saying and I wanted to straighten him out and remind him that it *did* carry on. So I'm simply doing what you do for me," John said, turning to Yoko. "And that's why we like to do interviews together," he continued, now turning to me, "because sometimes we forget things about our own work, and we

need to remind each other . . . And dear," John observed to Yoko, "another thing that's going to throw you: in his 'Concept Art' essay, Henry Flynt's talking about the song 'Sweets for My Sweet' by the Drifters . . . so he's been rocking for a long time! 'Sweets for my Sweet' was a big rock-'n'-roll hit—'Sweets for my sweet, sugar for my honey'—so he's been aware of that for a long time. I don't think he got to that sound pissing about with mathematics . . . So I'm sorry, but I had to interrupt, but I've been reading his essay about concept art, and it's bloody hard, but he gets to 'Sweets for My Sweet' and I finally understood him."

"Probably I was the only one who didn't," Yoko responded caustically.

"Dun de dun-dun!" John teased her. "I'm not putting you down, dear, I'm just very surprised to read this."

"I know you mean well," Yoko replied, "but I've now forgotten what I was saying to Jonathan."

"I think you were talking about the 4/4 beat," John said.

"Yes, Jonathan, what I was saying before about thinking that the 1–2–3–4 pop beat was kind of simplistic, because I was still doing my Music of the Mind . . . well, suddenly I realized that the *heartbeat* is 1–2, 1–2."

"You have to do it intellectually, is what she's saying," John teased her again.

"Well, all right," Yoko said with a sigh. "But I realized that modern classical composers, when they went from 4/4 to 4/3, lost the heartbeat. It's as if they lifted off from the ground and went to live on the fortieth floor. Arnold Schoenberg and Anton Webern—Webern's on the top of the Empire State Building. But that's all right. I still carry on the conceptual rhythm with my voice, and there's even a very complicated rhythm in my song 'Why,' but the bass and the drum are the heartbeat. And these days I'm putting a beat under everything I do."

"At the beginning of your relationship," I asked John, "did you ever get slightly intimidated about Yoko's talent and forthrightness?"

"Well, we've clashed artistically," John said with a laugh. "Our egos have smashed once or twice. But if I know what I'm doing as a male and as an artist, then I can see if I'm being hypocritical in my reactions. And if I find that I am, I stop. I sometimes am overawed by her talent. I think, fuck, I better watch out, she *is* taking over, I better get meself in here. And I say, Are you going to take over? And she'll say, No, no, no! And then I'll say, all right, all right, and I relax again."

"You see," Yoko explained, "both of us are extremely tough and extremely vulnerable. And if I get upset it's when I see that he's an extremely tough man. But then I have to remember that John's vulnerable, too. Because he gets scared—"

"Yeh," said John, "I think she's going to haul 365 legs [for the film *Up Your Legs Forever*] and make a bloody film about a fly crawling over some woman's body [*Fly*], what is it? And what am I supposed to do? But it's all right, I know her."

"An artist couple is the most difficult thing," Yoko continued. "On the David Frost television program, some guy was saying, 'I like to write music and my fiancée likes to write poetry.' And David Frost said, 'Well, you're lucky that she likes to write poetry and not music. Because if she wanted to write music, wouldn't that be a problem?' But the fact is that both John and I paint, compose, sing, write poetry, and make films, and on that basis I think we're doing remarkably well."

"If you do two LP records there might be a little change!" John told her, laughing. "But until then I don't mind. When she wants the A side, that's when I'm in trouble . . . And do you know the reason why the covers of our two Plastic Ono Band albums are similar?" he asked me.

"I noticed that on both of them you're both lying under a tree with the light falling around you. On her cover, she's reclining on your lap, but on your cover, you're reclining on *her* lap."

"Right," John told me. "And that's because I wanted us to be separate and to be together, too, not to have it appear that John and Yoko is over, because they're dying for us to fall apart, for God knows what reason. It's just that everybody doesn't want anybody else to be happy, because nobody's happy."

"I think it's a miracle that we're doing all right," Yoko

136

said quietly. "But we are doing all right, don't you think so, John?"

"It's just handy to fuck your best friend, that's all," he answered. "That's what it is. And once I resolved the fact that it was a woman as well, it was all right. Because I never really had any woman *friends* before. We go through the trauma of life and death together every day, so it's not so much of a worry what sex we are anymore. You know, I now understand the difference between sex and wanting me mother, which is a *big* trip. Promiscuity, in a nutshell, is wanting your mother, wanting *all* the mummies in the world. Want want want! I'm not living with a woman who I just lay and who's only got a pretty face. I'm living with an artist who's sparking me and inspiring me night and day to work."

"Do you have any sisters, Yoko?" I said to her jokingly.

"I *do*, by the way [*laughing*], and she's a pretty lady."

"And you know, Yoko is the most famous unknown artist," John continued. "Everybody knows her name, but nobody knows what she does . . .

"Well, it's after midnight now," John informed me as he glanced at his watch. "So why don't you come back tomorrow. I'll be around, but you could talk just to Yoko about her work and find out what she's been up to all her life!"

And when I returned to the Regency Hotel the next afternoon, I did just that.

. . .

Yoko Ono was born in Tokyo on February 18, 1933, the eldest of three children. Her mother, Isoko, was the granddaughter of Zenjiro Yasuda, one of Japan's most famous merchant princes and the founder of the Yasuda Bank; he was assassinated by a right-wing ultranationalist youth in 1921. Her father, Eisuke Ono—a descendant of a ninth-century Japanese emperor—was also a banker who, as a young man, had been an accomplished classical pianist. Their home was located on a hill behind the grounds of the Imperial Palace and commanded a sweeping view of the city. In an autobiographical essay that Yoko wrote for the Japanese magazine *Bungei Shunju* in 1974, she mentions that her father was always overseas on business trips, and that her mother spent much of her time socializing with friends in Tokyo. "There were several maids and private tutors beside me," Yoko writes. "I had one private tutor who read me the Bible and another foreign tutor who gave me piano lessons, and my attendant taught me Buddhism. . . . I had every meal by myself, alone. I was told the meal was ready and went into the dining room, where there was a long table for me to eat at. My private tutor watched me silently, sitting on the chair beside me."

But when she was twelve years old, Yoko found herself huddling with her mother and younger brother and sister in an underground bunker as American B-29s firebombed Tokyo on March 9, 1945, killing more than eighty thousand and incinerating a quarter of the city. Yoko's father had been working since 1942 in Hanoi as a manager of Japan's largest foreign exchange bank in French Indochina—he was also imprisoned for a time in a Chinese-run prison camp in Saigon—so Yoko's mother took refuge with her three children in a rural farming village where she and Yoko would haul their belongings about in a wheelbarrow and barter expensive kimonos and other family possessions, such as a German-made sewing machine, for rice and vegetables. Although Yoko went about in *monpe* (coarse farmer's trousers) and carried a rucksack on her back, she was constantly teased by the local children for "smelling like butter" (*bata kusai*)—their way of branding her as a Westernized city girl. So Yoko found refuge in daydreams. In a 1992 exhibition catalog essay entitled "SKYTALK with love to Denmark," she mused: "I started to love just lying down on the tatami and watching the sky. . . . It was so high and bright that you felt faint and exhilarated at the same time. Since then, all my life, I have been in love with the sky. Even when everything was falling apart around me, the sky was always there for me. . . . As I told myself then . . . I can never give up on life as long as the sky is there." Many years later, in her song "Watching the Rain," she would sing: "Let the blue sky heal you."

After the war, Yoko attended the elite Gakushuin, or Peers' School (the equivalent of Eton), where her schoolmates included Emperor Hirohito's two sons—the crown prince and present emperor, Akihito, and his younger brother,

Prince Yoshi, who apparently developed a schoolboy crush on her—as well as the internationally acclaimed novelist Yukio Mishima, who would later denounce Emperor Hirohito for renouncing his claim of divinity at the end of World War II. At the end of his life, Mishima embraced Bushido—the code of the samurai warrior-knight—and committed ritual suicide by seppuku after failing to inspire a coup d'etat in 1970. In his novel *Runaway Horses*, he wrote: "Perfect purity is possible if you turn your life into a line of poetry written with a splash of blood."

"I actually knew Mishima," Yoko informed me. "He'd gone to my school, and later he became a kind of a pop star like Mick Jagger and was part of the most raving, swinging circle in Japan. His writing was brilliant and a bit like Oscar Wilde's. A flamboyant guy. And when I was back in Japan one time, there was a big dinner party that was attended by a lot of celebrities. I was sitting directly across from him, but he refused to acknowledge me. John Cage was sitting next to me on one side and Peggy Guggenheim on the other side, and Mishima was talking to both of them—in very fluent English, by the way—but he just looked up at the ceiling and never said a word to me the entire dinner. It was a very unnatural situation. And then he put the rumor out that I was just one of those Westernized Japanese scarlet women, which was a very destructive thing for my happenings and events because he was very influential. But I didn't know he was that crazy. It was such a pity that this really brilliant writer killed himself."

Yoko graduated from Gakushuin in 1951. A year later, she was the first female ever to be accepted as a philosophy student at its associated Gakushuin University, but she dropped out after two semesters. Her father had been appointed director of the Bank of Tokyo in New York City, and the nineteen-year-old Yoko joined her family in Scarsdale, New York, and enrolled at Sarah Lawrence College in nearby Bronxville. Her Gakushuin classmate, Prince Yoshi, regretted her departure and sent Yoko an autographed picture of himself, accompanied by a poem he had composed especially for her: "Let us ask the high wave from far away / If the person I dream of is safe or not." As Yoko would later remark to me, "I felt that he was such an incredibly pure spirit. Everyone knew that he was kind of attached to my spirit, and every morning and every night he would pray that I would be well."

When I was going to Sarah Lawrence," Yoko told me when I visited her at the Regency Hotel, "I was mainly staying in the music library and listening to the music of Arnold Schoenberg and Anton Webern . . . they thrilled me, really. And I was writing some serial works at that time. But I was lazy when it came to writing out a whole score. And further, I was doing my *Lighting Piece* in those days, just lighting a match and watching until it disappeared. And I even thought that maybe there was something in me that was going to go crazy, like a pyromaniac. See, I was writing poetry and music and painting, and none of that satisfied me. Somehow I knew that the medium was wrong. Whenever I wrote a poem, they said it was too long, it was like a short story. A novel was like a short story, and a short story was like a poem. An opera sounded like a song, and a song sounded like an opera. I felt that I was like a misfit in every medium. But then I thought that there might be some people who needed something more than painting, poetry, and music, something I called an 'additional act' that you needed in life. And I was doing all that just to prevent myself from going mad, really. That's how I felt."

In 1955, she dropped out after three years at Sarah Lawrence, moved to Manhattan, and eloped with a remarkable young Japanese composer, who was a student of John Cage, named Toshi Ichiyanagi. Although they were married for six years, the couple lived apart for much of that time, but remained artistic collaborators, in both New York and Tokyo. As Yoko confided to the art curator Alexandra Munroe, "The pressure of becoming a Yasuda/Ono was so tremendous—intellectual, social, academic, and bourgeois pressure. Unless I rebelled against it I wouldn't have survived."

"My new life was very exciting," Yoko recounted to me. "I was living around Eighty-sixth Street and Amsterdam Avenue, next to a meat market, and I felt as if I had a house with a delicatessen in it. The only thing that I couldn't figure out was how to present my work because I didn't know how to communicate with people. And I didn't know how to explain to people how shy I was. When people visited, I wanted to be in a big sort of box with little holes where nobody could see me but I could see through the holes. So, later, that developed into my *Bag Piece*, where you can be inside and see outside, but they can't see you. And when I finally had my new apartment in New York, what happened was that instead of drying my face with a towel, I used the best cocktail dress that I used to wear at Sarah Lawrence. And then I was imagining myself all the time as a kite, and when I was sleeping, I'd lose my string, go off floating. So I just imagined myself holding on to a kite, and the kite was *me*. That's the time I thought: I'll go crazy.

"People asked me what I was doing. I didn't know how to explain that actually I was just holding the string, making sure that I wouldn't let go. This was a trait I had when I was a little girl, too, when my mother asked me what I was doing all by myself, and I would say 'I'm breathing,' and I was really counting my breathings, and thinking 'My God, if I don't count them, would I not breathe?' And that later became my *Breath Piece*."

"Draw a line with yourself," Yoko once wrote in her *Line Piece III*. "Go on drawing until you disappear." Many of Yoko's pieces were collected in her book *Grapefruit*, published in 1964 and consisting of a series of Zen koan–like instructional poems and "event scores" that the critic David

Bourdon called "one of the monuments of conceptual art of the early 1960s," and furthermore declared that the book exemplified "a lyrical, poetic dimension that sets her apart from the other conceptual artists." But as Yoko confessed to me, *Grapefruit* was in fact "a cure for myself without my knowing it. It was like saying, 'Please accept me, I am mad.' Those instructions are like that—a real need to do something to act out your madness. As long as you are behaving properly, you don't realize your madness and you go crazy."

In October 1960, and financially on her own, Yoko rented a large loft at 112 Chambers Street in downtown New York. "All the windows were smoked glass," she told me, "so that you couldn't really see outside, so it was dark and dingy, but there was the skylight, and when you were in the loft you almost felt more connected to the sky than to the city outside. It was beautiful. And it was a cold-water flat, $50.50 a month, and it was just great. I didn't have chairs or beds, and so the people downstairs gave me orange crates, and I put all the crates together to make a large table, and crates for the chairs, and at night I just collected them and made a bed out of them and would sleep on that. Then someone else gave me a huge heater, which was a luxury for me, and I started to live there. In those days there weren't very many people living in lofts in that area, so when the cops saw the lights on upstairs, they'd come up to ask how I was doing and if everything was all right. And I'd have to pretend that I was just working late because I wasn't supposed to be living there.

"I rented a baby grand piano, and a friend of mine told me that there was a group of artists who were thinking of finding somewhere where they could put on their works and would I mind if they joined with me and did things together. And I said I wouldn't mind, but in exchange, perhaps they wouldn't mind painting my loft for free. I thought that would be great, but everyone was sort of lazy and didn't get around to painting it white. But I got used to the gray, and I began to think that it was more interesting."

The legendary Chambers Street loft concerts featured artists, musicians, dancers, poets, and filmmakers, a list of whose names reads like a roster of the avant-garde Hall of Fame: George Maciunas, Walter De Maria, La Monte Young, Jackson Mac Low, Philip Corner, George Brecht, Yvonne Rainer, Henry Flynt, David Tudor, Jonas Mekas, and Richard Maxfield. "But there was no mention that *I* should have a concert there, and I wasn't going to be the one to mention it," Yoko told me. "Somehow my work was still suffering. The idea had been to stop my suffering by getting a place to present my work and at last letting everybody know what I was doing. But it just went on like that. Many people thought that I was a very rich girl who was just 'playing avant-garde,' even though my family wasn't sending me any money. And some others thought that I was the mistress of some very rich man, which wasn't true either. And I think that the reason that some people thought the whole thing was organized by some Chinese man was because

La Monte's last name was Young. So I was just surviving by teaching Japanese folk art."

Yoko's first solo art exhibition, which featured her *Instruction Paintings*, took place in July 1961 at the AG Gallery on Madison Avenue, which was co-owned by Fluxus originator George Maciunas. (Fluxus was the name of a group of Zen-, Dada-, and John Cage–influenced avant-garde artists who often worked in mixed media, and which, as Maciunas once wrote, expressed "the fusion of Spike Jones, Vaudeville, gag, children's games, and Duchamp.") "Before my exhibition," Yoko told me, "I went to look at the gallery, and I thought, Wow, he must be rich to have such a great gallery! But it turned out that he wasn't paying the rent, and he couldn't even pay the electricity bill. By the time my show went on, there was no electricity and we couldn't have an opening in the evening because it would be too dark, so it took place during the day instead.

"I was expecting a fantastic opening," Yoko said. "And I actually wore a cocktail dress as opposed to just pants and a sweater. And then I waited. But it was July, and only five people showed up: John Cage, Isamu Noguchi, a girl who was living with me at the time, and Beate Gordon and her daughter." Beate Sirota Gordon, who was then the performing arts director of the Japan Society, had arranged for Yoko to present calligraphy, sumi painting, and origami demonstrations at several colleges. Gordon, who has a truly remarkable life story, had spent her childhood in Tokyo where her Ukrainian-born father, who had emigrated with his family to Japan, had been Yoko's piano teacher before the war. At the age of twenty-two, she was chosen to be a member of the committee that wrote the post–World War II Japanese Constitution, and she had an integral role in drafting the women's rights section that provided for legal equality between men and women.

Among Yoko's *Instruction Paintings* on display were *Painting for the Wind*, which consisted of a canvas bag filled with seeds hanging in front of a blank canvas, so that when the wind blew, seeds would fall out through the bag's small hole; *Smoke Painting*, in which the viewer was instructed to light a canvas with a match and watch the smoke make ever-shifting rising and curling patterns against it until the canvas was consumed; *Painting to Be Stepped On*, which was created as people stepped on a torn piece of linen lying on the gallery floor and covered it with footprint marks; and *Shadow Painting*, in which a blank canvas, positioned near a window, "came to life" when shadows were cast on it—suggesting the haunting lines from Shakespeare's fifty-third sonnet: "What is your substance, whereof are you made, / That millions of strange shadows on you tend?"

Yoko's first major public solo concert of her experimental compositions took place on November 24, 1961, at Carnegie Recital Hall. "It was a big moment for me," she recalled. "George Brecht, Jonas Mekas, La Monte Young, Jackson Mac Low, just about everyone performed in it. And Richard Maxfield helped me on the electronic side, and I set up everything and then made the stage very dim, so you had to strain your eyes—because life is like that. You always have to strain to read other people's minds. It was very vaguely lit, and then it went into complete darkness. One guy was sleeping on the floor of the stage, and I put live crickets around the hall. The week before I had given instructions to everyone as to what they should do, so that there would be a feeling of togetherness based on alienation, since no one knew the other person's instructions.

"So everybody was moving without making any sounds onstage. There was a point where two men were tied up together with lots of empty cans and bottles around them, and they had to move from one end of the stage to the other very quietly and very slowly—it took about forty minutes to go back and forth—without making any sounds."

"Did the audience understand what you were trying to do?" I asked.

"No," she said, "and after the concert one of the dancers even told me, 'You know, people complained that they couldn't even see me because it was too dark'—some prima-donna remark like that [*laughing*]."

"Little children," I mentioned, "are often scared of the dark and hear things that aren't there and want the bedroom door to be slightly ajar while they're sleeping."

"Yes," Yoko agreed, "because I'm basically a child who's afraid and who can't communicate and wants to commu-

148

nicate. As I mentioned to you last night, before I speak I stutter in my mind, like 'O-O-Oh-h-ho-how are you I-I-want-to-know-wh-wh-what's going on.' And then my cultured self tries to correct that stutter into a clean sentence, so that it comes out like 'Oh, and how are *you* today?' But before it comes out like that I have that stuttering in me. And I wanted to deal with those sounds of people's fears and stutterings.

"So I thought that if everything was set up in a lighted room and suddenly the light was turned off, you might start to see things beyond the shapes. Or hear the kind of sounds that you hear in silence. You would start to feel the environment and tension and people's vibrations. Those were the sounds that I wanted to deal with, the sound of fear and of darkness, like a child's fear that someone is behind him, but he can't speak and communicate this. And so I asked one guy to stand behind the audience for the duration of the concert.

"I wanted the sound of people perspiring to be in it, too, so I had all the dancers wear contact microphones, and the instructions were to bring out very heavy boxes and take them back across the stage, and while they were doing that the dancers were perspiring a little. And there was somebody standing in the toilet throughout the evening. Whenever I go to a toilet in a film theater, I always feel very scared. If nobody's there I'm scared, but if somebody is there it's even more scary. So I wanted people to have that experience of fear. There are unknown areas of sound and experience that people can't really mention in words. I was interested not in the noise you make but the noise that happens when you try not to make it, just that tension going back and forth.

"I think I would never want to go back again to where I was, doing things like that, even though few people have touched this area. Where I'd be so lonely and miserable that nobody understood. And the kind of thing I'm doing now is more understandable. I'm not saying it's better or worse. But now I just want to feel sort of playful sometimes. And when I feel playful, to do something. That's when people seem to understand more, or at least accept more."

Following Leo Tolstoy's injunction to "make it strange," Yoko's events, poems, paintings, sculptures, photographs, music, and films all exhibit and celebrate a sense of child-like playfulness and wonderment, a way of seeing things as if you were entering a strange street, invisible until now, for the first time, or as if, for example, you were watching a western—the sheriff, rustlers, corral fights—through the eyes of one of the horses. In her beautiful "Touch Poem," Yoko writes: "Give birth to a child. / See the world through its eye. / Let it touch everything possible / and leave its fin- germark there / in place of a signature." And this poem is itself one of Yoko's signature statements, perfectly encapsu- lating and defining her aesthetic creed as well as her way of experiencing the world.

In a mesmerizing twenty-five-minute film that she made in late 1970, Yoko actually observes the world through the spherical compound eyes of a fly. The "world" in this film entitled *Fly* is a naked woman lying recumbent and comatose on a bed; and we watch a fly in huge close-ups (although about two hundred insects were used in the film, at least one for every take) crawling, climbing, perching, nestling, delving, tasting, and even, it sometimes appears, praying on toes, fingertips, lips, ears, armpits, nipples, vagina—ceaselessly exploring the dunelike crescents and curves of this corporeal Saharan landscape.

At the film's conclusion, there is an extraordinary long shot of six flies resting as if expectantly on the motionless woman's body. Seeing this image, I was reminded of a haiku written by the eighteenth-century Japanese poet Issa: "Go ahead— / Make love, my flies. / I'm leaving now." And after a moment, the flies fly away, and the camera shifts focus with a shot through the window behind her onto a Bowery rooftop, the sky veiled in a diaphanous blue light like Saint Elmo's fire.

"The idea for *Fly* came to me," Yoko remarked, "when I thought about that joke where someone says to a man 'Did you notice that woman's hat?' and he's looking at her bosom instead. I wondered how many people would look at the fly or at the body. I tried, when filming, to accept all the things that showed up, but at the same time tried not to make the film too dramatic. It would have been very easy for me to have made it become pornographic, and I didn't want that. Each shot had to project more than a pretty image of a body, so it was used more as an abstract line." But when introducing the film at the 1971 Cannes Film Festival, Yoko told the audience: "Everyone is that female, just lying down, just taking it."

Yoko's soundtrack for *Fly* is one of her most subtle and fantastical performances. She created it with John in the bedroom of their Regency Hotel suite over the 1970 Christmas weekend. John had suggested that they "knock it off before the ten o'clock news," and while operating a Nagra tape recorder, he recorded Yoko's solo vocal performance in one take, to which he later overlaid a forward and reverse guitar track.

Although Yoko improvised her soundtrack without looking at the film, a fly's spirit must have taken inexorable possession of her soul that night, for one uncannily experiences her voice as if it were a kind of vocal oscilloscope, instantaneously registering the barely perceptible, hair-trigger beats of a fly's antennae, legs, and wings, as well as of its circumscribed but vertiginous flight patterns. "It's nice to go into that very very fine, intricate mixture of sounds and rhythms," Yoko remarked to me. "It's almost like going into a dream, getting something that doesn't exist in the physical world, unutterable sounds—a kind of metaphysical rhythm." In his book *The World of Silence*, the Swiss philosopher Max Picard proposes that "music is silence, which in dreaming begins to sound," and adds, in a very Onoesque manner: "In silence the lines of the mouth are like the closed wings of a

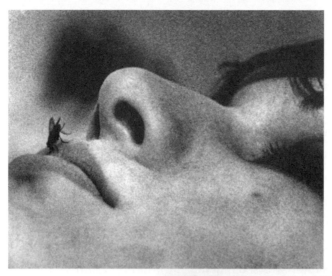

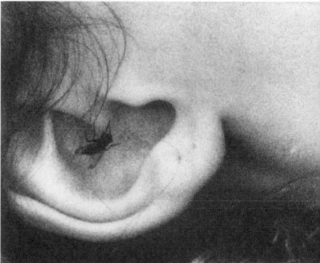

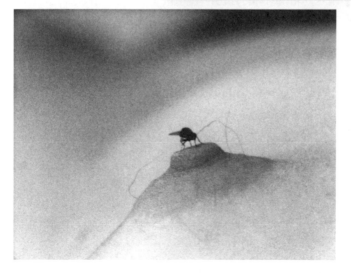

butterfly. When the word starts moving, the wings open, and the butterfly flies away."

"Around the time that I met John," Yoko told me at the conclusion of our conversation, "I went to a palmist—John would probably laugh at this—and he said, 'You're like a very, very fast wind that goes speeding around the world.' And I had a line that signified astral projection. The only thing I didn't have was a root. But, the palmist said, you've met a person who's fixed like a mountain, and if you get connected with that mountain you might get materialized. And John is like a frail wind, too, so he understands all these aspects. I'm starting to think that maybe I can live. Before it seemed impossible—I was just about at the vanishing point, and all my things were too conceptual. But John came in and said, 'All right, I understand you.' And just by saying that, all those things that were supposed to vanish stayed."

John and Yoko flew back to London after the Christmas holiday, but returned to New York in early March 1971. John's previous crush on the city had developed into a serious affair—he came, he saw, and he was conquered. "If I'd lived in Roman times," he declared, "I'd have lived in Rome. Where else? Today America is the Roman Empire and New York is Rome itself." New York also reminded him of the City of Light. "It's beginning to look like Paris when

I was younger, when I was twenty-four," he said, "and when people were holding hands and kissing under bridges. It's happening again. People are dreaming again." But he may have been wearing rose-colored glasses when he compared New York to the imaginary little Welsh seaside village of Llareggub (whose name is best understood read backward) that Dylan Thomas wrote about in his radio play *Under Milk Wood*—a cockled-cobbled hamlet of the heart's desire where "You can hear the dew falling, and the hushed town breathing. Only your eyes are unclosed to see the black and folded town fast, and slow, asleep."

But, as John once confessed, he actually needed to live somewhere that was "alive and kicking continually," and for him, New York was Liverpool redivivus. "There's the same quality of energy, of vitality, in both cities," he remarked. "New York is at my speed. It's a twenty-four-hours-a-day city, it's going on around you all the time, so much so that you almost stop noticing it. But it's all there if you want it: the telephone can bring you anything and everything." He and Yoko went about the city undisturbed, and taxi drivers treated him as one of the locals. Moreover, as he once told a BBC reporter, "I can go right out this door now and go in a restaurant. You want to know how great that is?" And astonished New Yorkers would occasionally catch sight of both of them riding around town on the bicycles they had purchased—hers a high-tech Japanese model, and his styled after a classic Raleigh Lenton Sports bike.

I would occasionally run into John and Yoko at odd times and places. One afternoon, a friend of mine and I walked into Serendipity 3, a landmark sweetshop-cum-restaurant-cum-boutique that had been frequented in the past by movie stars such as Marilyn Monroe and Bette Davis. Located in a town house on Manhattan's Upper East Side and filled with oversize Victorian posters and Tiffany lamps, the restaurant was known for its lemon icebox pie and frozen hot chocolates, and offered dishes such as Bi-Sensual Burgers and a Madame Butterfly Pasta. That afternoon, my friend and I suddenly noticed John and Yoko huddled over a small corner table, with no one paying them any mind, looking just like two lovers speaking softly and whispering sweet nothings. But when they noticed us, they waved us over to share frozen hot chocolates with them.

About a month later, John and Yoko invited me to join them for a dinner at the Upper West Side apartment of one of Yoko's old friends from the early 1960s so that they could bring me up to date on what they had been doing in the city. It was the evening of March 17, 1971, and for the occasion, John was wearing a military olive-green, short-sleeved shirt with wide pockets and yellow epaulets. John and Yoko asked me to sit between them at the table. Over a dinner of fish and white wine, the three of us—for the most part unmindful of the rest of the guests—talked the evening away, and throughout the meal I felt like nothing so much as a tennis net over which a series of rapid conversational volleys between John and Yoko were being unleashed, constantly reminding me that although in tennis scoring "love" means nothing, with John and Yoko it meant everything.

The following is an account of the match:

ME: Have you both been having a good time in New York?

JOHN: Yeh, great!

ME: What have you been doing?

YOKO: Well, we've been meeting all the people we've been wanting to meet.

JOHN: Jerry Rubin, Abbie Hoffman, Frank Zappa—

YOKO: And David Peel [the legendary Lower East Side gadfly street musician whose songs include "Everybody's Smoking Marijuana," "I'm Gonna Start Another Riot," and the notorious "The Pope Smokes Dope"].

JOHN: I watched him in Washington Square Park last Sunday. And just today we were walking down Second Avenue near the Fillmore East, and we ran into him with his acoustic guitar on the street singing "The Pope Smokes Dope."

ME: Did you both join in?

JOHN: Yeh, sure. He started to sing and we started to harmonize.

YOKO: I said, "Let's Peel It Together!" And gradually a lot of people began to walk with us and joined in.

JOHN: We walked along for about five minutes singing

"mari-marijuana" just like Pied Pipers. Until we were moved on by the police! It was very nice.

YOKO: And the other day we went to have dinner with Andy Warhol. When I first met John, he asked me what kind of person Andy Warhol was. So I said he was one of the most sensitive people I'd ever met. And John didn't believe it because Andy projects this image of tough-ness. Just like us, you know. But he's not like that at all. So Andy, John, and I had dinner, and I guess we must have really looked like three freaks sitting together. Andy kept saying to me, Listen, Yoko, you used to make a film a day, you used to be a hard worker, you've got to start working!

JOHN: Little does he know! And Andy's taken us to many great shops.

YOKO: Yes, we've gone shopping and bought a lot of clothes. And these days we feel very good because when we get up, we feel very thankful that we have some clothes to wear. You know, like last year, we just wore one thing—

JOHN: Just two pairs of overalls and two shirts for the year.

ME: Since I saw you a few months ago you seem to have lost a lot of weight. How did you do it?

YOKO: I hope, Jonathan, that you might note that we've lost *twenty pounds* this year. This is one thing very worth reporting. I think that we're looking rather attractive for a middle-aged couple! [*Laughing*]

ME: It's noted. How did you happen to lose weight?

JOHN: We worried! [*Laughing*]

YOKO: And Andy also took us to an antique market—

JOHN: Where I got an old Mickey Mouse watch and a nice antique plastic radio that's horribly yellow and green.

YOKO: And some plastic rings that Andy Warhol selected for me.

JOHN: And a Pat Boone bag that says YOUR PAL, PAT BOONE.

YOKO: And we found a place in the Village where a guy makes name badges on the spot. Have you seen that?

ME: No.

JOHN: Well, he takes a Polaroid, then he cuts it out and puts it into what looks like a potato masher that just goes sha-*joooop*, and you have a badge.

YOKO: He made us a JOHN AND YOKO badge, and we said thank you, can we pay for it? And he said no. Everyone is giving us things for free.

JOHN: And the kids we've met on the street have been giving us candles and T-shirts. It's beautiful.

ME: You should consider running for office.

JOHN: Not yet. [*Laughing*] You know, I've also been down to the Department of Immigration trying to get an extension for our visas!

YOKO: And we've been going out and eating at Serendipity and Nathan's and a Japanese restaurant on Eighth Street. Also Max's Kansas City, which is going to do a charity show of art objects, and we're going to be in it, too. I take John around the city and say to him, Oh, I

159

used to live here, John, did you know that? And then we
go somewhere else and I tell him, And *this* is where I
used to live. And there are about fifty places like that, so
John is going crazy.

JOHN: We went to Broadway to see *Lenny* and also to *Oh!
Calcutta!* because I had a piece in it. But it was awful.
The show was terrible.

YOKO: And we showed some of our films at the Museum of
Modern Art . . . and when we go back to England, we're
going to make a film to accompany John's new album.

JOHN: It will show us at home in the garden with the
geese—

YOKO: And all the rooms in the house.

JOHN: You see, we just made an album in our home studio
[in Tittenhurst Park] with George [Harrison], Jim
Keltner, Nicky Hopkins, Klaus Voormann, Jim Gordon,
different people on each track.

ME: What are some of the song titles?

JOHN: The title of one's going to be called "Imagine." And
Yoko co-wrote one of the tracks. It's one of the best on
the album.

ME: What's it called?

JOHN: "Oh My Love." [*Sings*] "Oh my love, for the first
time in my life / My eyes are wide open." It's very
sweet. I hope you'll like it. And Yoko designed the
cover—it's going to be my face with just clouds instead
of eyes.

YOKO: And also in the oven is a film we want to make
    together called *In Your Own Grapefruit*, which is my
    book *Grapefruit* and John's *In His Own Write* combined
    together.

ME: My own copy of *Grapefruit* is in tatters.

YOKO: It's very precious now.

ME: I know.

JOHN: You can get ten dollars for that now in London!

YOKO: No, thirty dollars, John! Thirty dollars! [*Laughing*]

ME: It sounds like you're having a great time.

JOHN: Yeh, it's been a star-studded story [*laughing*], and it's
    been great fun, really groovy. It's nice to blast in some-
    where. And I love the Village.

YOKO: I thought it might have been nice after dinner if we
    all went on the Staten Island Ferry because John's never
    done that. But it's getting late, so maybe we can do that
    another time.

ME: You should come back more often.

JOHN: We will do.

YOKO: John and I are very close to each other—we suddenly
    found out! [*Laughing*] We're very happy about that.

JOHN: And that's our whole life.

YOKO: In five minutes!

JOHN: And now we're here!

. . .

Two months later, a friend of mine and I had gone to see *Carnal Knowledge*, which was having its New York premiere at an Upper East Side cinema, and afterward we bumped into John and Yoko in the lobby. Accompanied by the Yippie activist Jerry Rubin and one of his fellow travelers, they invited us to Ratner's restaurant on the Lower East Side for blintzes—"that's why we go there," John informed us—where a beatific, long-haired young man approached our table and wordlessly handed John a card inscribed with a pithy saying of the inscrutable Meher Baba (the self-proclaimed Indian Avatar of the Age who supposedly kept a forty-four-year vow of silence until his death) and walked back to his table. (Meher Baba communicated by means of an alphabet board, as well as by hand gestures that were interpreted and transmitted vocally by one of his disciples.) Rubin took one disparaging look at the card, drew a swastika on the back of it, and delivered it to the avatar's emissary. When the gloating Rubin returned, John admonished him gently, suggesting that this wasn't the way to change someone's consciousness. As far as I was concerned, an audible avatar was sitting just beside me, and his sung and spoken message of peace, love, and understanding was one that could be heard around the world.

In July 1971, John and Yoko returned to England in order to promote a new edition of Yoko's book *Grapefruit* and gave a press conference at the Apple Corps headquarters in Savile Row, during which John remarked: "In England

I'm regarded as the lucky guy who won the pools. Yoko's regarded as the lucky Jap who married the guy who won the pools. In America, we are both treated as artists." John and Yoko realized that the time had inevitably come for both of them to bid farewell to England, and at the beginning of September, they packed up some of their belongings and moved to New York City. After staying at the St. Regis Hotel for several weeks, they rented a small, two-bedroom duplex apartment at 105 Bank Street in Greenwich Village—John had at long last gotten back to where he knew he had always belonged. John Cage—Yoko's friend and collaborator from her Fluxus days—lived next door; Bob Dylan had taken up residence with his family on nearby MacDougal Street; and around the corner was the legendary White Horse Tavern whose customers over the years had included Dylan Thomas, Jack Kerouac, James Baldwin, Jim Morrison, and Hunter S. Thompson.

In 1912, the bohemian art patron Mabel Dodge—a friend of D. H. Lawrence and Gertrude Stein—turned her Greenwich Village apartment at Fifth Avenue and Ninth Street into a salon where radical luminaries like John Reed, Emma Goldman, and Margaret Sanger assembled to share their revolutionary dreams. Sixty years later, and just ten blocks away, John and Yoko similarly turned their own West Village apartment into a meeting place for political activists, musicians, artists, writers, and photographers who, in a manner reminiscent of the Bed-Ins for Peace, gathered around their bed—an almost room-size mattress resting on two dark wooden church pews—and talked until the wee hours about how they, too, might be able to change the world.

For the next couple of months—and in spite of the looming threat of having their visas revoked—John and Yoko threw caution to the wind and fearlessly took part in a number of political protests. They attended a demonstration in Syracuse, New York, on behalf of the Native American Onondaga tribe, as well as one in New York City to protest the Bogside Massacre of thirteen Catholic civil rights demonstrators by British soldiers in Northern Ireland; performed at a benefit concert at the Apollo Theater for the relatives of inmates slain at Attica prison; and, dressed in matching magenta T-shirts and leather jackets, appeared at the Ten for Two Freedom Rally in Ann Arbor, Michigan, to show support for John Sinclair, the founder of the White Panther Party, who was serving a ten-year prison sentence for having offered two marijuana joints to an undercover policewoman. At that rally, John Lennon sang his rousing song "John Sinclair" to his fifteen thousand supporters: "Let him be, set him free / Let him be like you and me." Three days after the concert, Sinclair was released on bail.

Six months later, John put out his album *Some Time in New York City*, which expressed musically what he and Yoko had been engaging in politically—"done in the tradition of minstrels," as John noted—and which included hard-core rock-'n'-roll agitprop songs like "John Sinclair," "Attica

State," and "Sunday Bloody Sunday," although the electrifying song "We're All Water," which was written and sung by Yoko, was in fact the album's highlight. As John told the British magazine *New Musical Express*, "Most other people express themselves by shouting or playing football at the weekend. But me, here am I in New York and I hear about the thirteen people shot dead in Ireland, and I react immediately. And being what I am, I react in four-to-the-bar with a guitar break in the middle. . . . The point, now, is that I want to say whatever it is I've got to say as simple as the music I like. And that's rock 'n' roll—and to match the lyrics to the music. So now it's 'A-WOP-BOP-A-LOO-BOP, GET OUTTA IRELAND!' "

Unbeknownst to John and Yoko, their Bank Street apartment was under FBI surveillance, their phones were bugged, and federal agents had been assigned to tail them. The 1972 presidential election was on the horizon, and Strom Thurmond, the segregationist and pro-war senator from South Carolina, had informed the Nixon White House that John, Yoko, and some of their radical friends were planning to disrupt that summer's Republican Party Convention in Miami. In February, John and Yoko's B-2 visas were about to expire, and in March, at the instigation of the attorney general's office, the Immigration and Naturalization Service "recalled" their visas and ordered John and Ono to leave the country by March 15. John fought the case—*U.S. vs. John Lennon*—through the courts for four-and-a-half years, and on October 7, 1975, the United States Court of Appeals reversed his deportation order, although he would have to wait another year to obtain his green card.

Ever since the night of May 19, 1968, when John and Yoko had initiated their romantic and artistic partnership, they had rarely been out of each other's sight for more than a few days. Deprived of Yoko's presence for even one hour, as John bemoaned in his song "Dear Yoko," "I wilt just like a fading flower." But in October 1973, having recently celebrated their fourth wedding anniversary and in the midst of their ongoing deportation court battle, the couple decided to separate. In fact, as John would later admit, "she kicked me out is what actually happened." Having committed a sexual indiscretion, John was sent packing to Los Angeles, and for a year and a half, he descended into a netherworld of sex, alcohol, and rock 'n' roll for what he famously described as his eighteen-month "lost weekend."

"Well, first I thought, Whoopee! Bachelor life! Whoopee, whoopee!" John would later confess to David Sheff. "And then I woke up one day and thought, What is this? I want to go home.... We were talking all the time on the phone, and I kept saying, 'I don't like this, I'm out of control. I'm drinking, I'm getting into trouble and I'd like to come home, please.' And she's saying, 'You're not ready to come home' ... and I keep calling, 'Can I come home yet?' 'You're not ready.' 'I'm ready.' 'No, you're not ready.' " For both of them it was a time to reenvision their lives. The novelist

Gabriel García Márquez, when asked about his thirty-year relationship with his wife, replied, "I know her so well now that I have not the slightest idea of who she really is." Sometimes couples who are inextricably enmeshed with each other find it necessary to create a space between themselves in order to reimagine their partnership. As John would later reflect on his and Yoko's separation: "That abandonment gave us the fulfillment we were looking for and the space to breathe and think and re-establish our dream"; and as he would later memorably remark, "Our separation was a failure." The couple reunited in January 1975, and on October 9, Yoko gave birth to their son, Sean Taro Ono Lennon. It was John's thirty-fifth birthday, and the proud New York City father declared: "I feel higher than the Empire State Building."

From 1975 until 1980, John and Yoko removed themselves from the world's gaze. To the public eye, they chose to be invisible; to the public ear, they elected to be silent. In an open letter to their fans and admirers, John and Yoko wrote: "Remember, we are writing in the sky instead of on paper—that's our song." As their close friend, the photographer Bob Gruen, would later poignantly remark, "People always say John gave up making music in this time, but really he didn't. He was just singing lullabies to his kid."

It has often been observed that life partners whose identities are inextricably attuned to each other are prone to unintentionally mirror each other's thoughts and feelings, and on hindsight, one might view much of John's and Yoko's work in this light. Yoko sang "Touch touch touch touch me love / Just one touch, touch will do," and John responded "Love is touch, touch is love." She exclaimed: "I said yes, I said yes, I said yes / I prayed a thousand times yes," and he concurred "Yes is the answer, and you know that for sure." Yoko instructed "Imagine the clouds dripping," and John proposed "Imagine there's no heaven." As a Beatle, John wrote "Tomorrow Never Knows" ("Turn off your mind, relax and float downstream / It is not dying, it is not dying"), and six years before John's death, Yoko eerily composed a song called "Tomorrow May Never Come" ("Yesterday may haunt us forever . . . Tomorrow may never come"). When I pointed out this thematic coincidence to Yoko years later, she told me, "I wasn't aware of that at all at that time, but both of us were on the same wavelength even when we didn't know it."

So on Friday, December 5, 1980, at seven in the evening, John and I sat down in Yoko's cloud-ceilinged office—he on her pearl-white couch and I on an adjoining white cushion chair. Yoko knocked on the door and brought in a cup of coffee for John and a cup of tea for me. After she left, he and I reminisced for a short while about the good old days in London when we had all first met at their Montagu Square flat in 1968, and at that moment I thought of Yoko's "Kite Song," in which she sings "That was a long time ago / Many skies went by since then." Now, twelve years later, I was with John and Yoko in their home in New York City, and as I glanced

heavenward to see the gossamer clouds hovering on the ceiling above me, John said, "O.K., I know you've got a Monday deadline, let's get boogieing!" So I removed a blank cassette tape from my shoulder bag, inserted it into my tape recorder, and pressed RECORD.

* * *

Double Fantasy *is the first recording you've made in five years, and, to quote from your song "The Ballad of John and Yoko," "It's good to have the both of you back."*

But the illusion that I was cut off from society is a joke. I was just the same as any of the rest of you, I was working from nine to five—baking bread and changing some nappies and dealing with the baby. People keep asking, "Why did you go underground, why were you hiding?" But I wasn't hiding. I went to Singapore, South Africa, Hong Kong, Bermuda. I've been everywhere in the bloody universe. I did everything—at least the kind of things that people who can afford to go to Singapore can do—and I did fairly average things, too . . . I went out to the movies.

Do you know how much was written about us during the so-calledfi ve years we weren't in the media? Reams and reams. We get the clippings from all over the world, so we have a vast overall picture of our impression on the public, not just in the rock business but on a worldwide scale.

The press coverage on John and Yoko when they were supposedly doing nothing for five years was immense.

But you weren't writing a lot of songs during those years.

I didn't write a damn thing . . . You know, it was a big
event for us to have a baby—people might forget how hard
we tried to have one and how many miscarriages we had
and near-death scenes for Yoko . . . and we actually had a
stillborn child and a lot of problems with drugs, a lot of
personal and public problems brought on by ourselves and
with help from our friends. But whatever. We put ourselves
in situations that were stressful, but we managed to have
the child that we tried to have for ten years, and my God,
we weren't going to blow it. We didn't *move* for a year, and I
took up yoga with the gray-haired lady on TV. [*Laughing*]
So we came through it all and were in a position where we
could afford to walk away from the so-called profession that
was earning us the money and could just be with the baby.

*You can't really win. People criticized you for not writing and
recording, but it's sometimes forgotten that your three previous
albums—*Some Time in New York City, Walls and Bridges,
and Rock 'n' Roll—*weren't universally praised . . . especially the
agitprop* Some Time in New York City, *which included songs
like "Attica State," "Sunday Bloody Sunday," and "Woman Is
the Nigger of the World."*

Yeh, that was the one that really upset everyone. Yoko calls it "Bertolt Brecht," but, as usual, I didn't know who he was until she took me to see Richard Foreman's production of *The Threepenny Opera* four years ago, and then I saw the album in that light. I was always irritated by the *rushness* of the sound on it, but I was consciously doing it like a newspaper where you get the misprints, the times and the facts aren't quite right, and there's that you've-got-to-get-it-out-by-Friday attitude.

But I've been attacked many, many times . . . and right from the beginning: "From Me to You" was "Below Par Beatles," don't forget that. That was the review in the *NME* [*New Musical Express*].

That's what they wrote?

Right. "Below Par Beatles." Jesus Christ, I'm *sorry*. Maybe it wasn't as good as "Please Please Me," I don't know, but "below par"? I'll never forget that one because it always struck me as interesting. And you know how bad the reviews were of our Plastic Ono albums? They shredded us! "Self-indulgent simplistic whining"—that was the main gist. It's the same assholes that booed Dylan for playing electric. Because those albums were about ourselves, you see, and not about Ziggy Stardust or Tommy. *Imagine* was accepted, but not the lyrics of the song, which they called "naïve" for trying to imagine there's no such things as countries or nationalities. And of course they reviewed

Walls and Bridges saying that it lacked the "solid reality" of "Mother" and "Working Class Hero" on my Plastic Ono album. And *Mind Games*, they *hated* it.

But it's not just *me*. Take Mick, for instance. Mick's put out consistently good work for twenty years, and will they give him a break? Will they ever say, "Look at him, he's number one, he's thirty-six and he's put out a beautiful song, 'Emotional Rescue.'" I enjoyed it, a lot of people enjoyed it. And God help Bruce Springsteen when they decide he's no longer God. I haven't seen him—I'm not a great "in"-person watcher—but I've heard such good things about him from people that I respect, and I might actually get out of bed to watch him. Right now his fans are happy. He's told them about being drunk and chasing girls and cars and everything, and that's about the level they enjoy. But when he gets down to facing his own success and growing older and having to produce it again and again, they'll turn on him, and I hope he survives it. All he has to do is look at me or at Mick. So it goes up and down, up and down—of course it does, but what are we, machines? What do they want from the guy, do they want him to kill himself onstage? Do they want me and Yoko to kill ourselves onstage? What would make the little turds happy? But when they criticized "From Me to You" as below par Beatles, that's when I first realized you've got to keep it up, there's some sort of system where you get on the wheel and you've got to keep going around.

Watching the wheels. What are those wheels?

The whole universe is a wheel, right? Wheels going round and round. They're my own wheels, mainly. But, you know, watching meself is like watching everybody else. And I watch meself through my child, too.

The thing about the child is . . . it's *still* hard. I'm not the greatest dad on earth, I'm doing me best. But I'm a very irritable guy, and I get depressed. I'm up and down, up and down, and he's had to deal with that, too—withdrawing from him and then giving, and withdrawing and giving. I don't know how much it will affect him in later life, but I've been *physically* there.

We're all selfish, but I think so-called artists are *completely* selfish: to put Yoko or Sean or the cat or anybody in mind other than meself—me and my ups and downs and my tiddly problems—is a strain. Of course, there's a reward and a joy, but still . . .

So you fight against your natural selfish instincts.

Yeh, the same as taking drugs or eating bad food or not doing exercise. It's as hard as that to give to a child, it's not natural at all. Maybe it's the way we were all brought up, but it's very hard to think about somebody else, even your own child, to *really* think about him.

But you're thinking about him in a song like "Beautiful Boy."

Yeh, but that's easy . . . it's *painting*. Gauguin was stuck in fucking Tahiti, painting a big picture for his daughter—if the movie version I saw was true, right? So he's in fucking Tahiti painting a picture for her, she dies in Denmark, she didn't see him for twenty years or something, he has VD and is going out of his mind in Tahiti—he dies and the painting gets burnt anyway, so nobody ever sees the masterpiece of his fucking life. And I'm always thinking things like that. So I write a song about the child, but it would have done better for me to spend the time I wrote the fucking song actually playing ball with him. The hardest thing for me to do is *play* . . . I can do everything else.

You can't play?

Play, I can't. I try and invent things, I can draw, I can watch TV with him. I'm great at that, I can watch any garbage, as long as I don't have to move around, and I can talk and read to him and go out and take him with me for a coffee and things like that.

That's weird, because your drawings and so many of the songs you've written are really playful.

That probably came from Paul more than from me.

What about "Good Morning Good Morning"? That's one of yours. It's a great song, a kind of playful day-in-the-life of this older guy who's roaming aimlessly around town after work because there's nothing happening and everything's closed and everyone's half asleep and he doesn't want to go home, so he takes a walk by his old school and starts checking out the girls and then goes to a show and has nothing to say but it's O.K.

Oh, that was just an exercise. I only had about a week to write songs for *Pepper.* "Good Morning Good Morning" was a Kellogg's Corn Flakes ad at the time—that's how desperate I was for a song.

What I realized when I read "Lennon Remembers" [the legendary 1970 interview with Jann Wenner] or the new *Playboy* interview [conducted by David Sheff in September 1980] was that I'm always complaining about how *hard* it is to write or how much I *suffer* when I'm writing—that almost every song I've ever written has been absolute torture.

Most of them were torture?

Absolutely. I always think there's nothing there, it's shit, it's no good, it's not coming out, this is garbage . . . and even if it does come out, I think, "What the hell is it anyway?"

That sounds a bit constipated, in a way.

It's just *stupid*. I just think, "That was tough, Jesus, I was in a bad way then." [*Laughing*] And then I realize that I've been saying that all these years about every session and every song, you know, except for the ten or so songs the gods give you and that come out of nowhere.

Did the songs you wrote for Double Fantasy *come easier?*

Not really, it actually took me five years for them to come out. Constipated for five years, and then diarrhea for three weeks! [*Laughing*] The physical writing was within a three-week period. There's a Zen story that Yoko once told me—and I think I might have told it in "Lennon Remembers" or "*Playboy* Forgets": A king sent his messenger to an artist to request a painting, he paid the artist the money, and the artist said, "O.K., come back." So a year goes by, and the messenger comes back and tells him, "The king's waiting for his painting," and the artist says, "Oh, hold on," and whips it off right in front of him and says, "Here." And the messenger says, "What's this? The king paid you twenty thousand bucks for this shit, and you knock it off in five minutes?" And the painter replies, "Yeah, but I spent ten years thinking about it." And there's no way I could have written the *Double Fantasy* songs without those five years.

· · ·

At this point, Yoko came into the room to announce that someone who said he was George Harrison had just telephoned and wanted to come over right away. "Of course it's not George," John muttered. "He was probably on acid," Yoko surmised. "I said to him, 'Can I ask you some questions?' 'No,' the guy said, 'I can't be bothered with all that, Yoko.' So I hung up and made a call to George's number and found out that George was in fact sleeping." I started to laugh, and John said, "We laugh at it, too, you know. Jesus Christ. If it wasn't a laugh, we'd go crazy, wouldn't we? And you know, all through our *Double Fantasy* sessions, we kept getting a constant flood of calls for Harry Nilsson, because people remembered I was with Harry seven years ago." [*Laughing*] "So how do you keep on keeping your sense of humor?" I asked him. "I live with Yoko!" John replied with a laugh.

Yoko took this opportunity to hand John a recent copy of Japanese *Playboy* that featured an article about them. "It's nice of them to show just the back of the baby," John remarked about one of the photos. "I don't want pictures of Sean going around. Most stars, as soon as they have a baby, put it on the front page: *We've just had a baby!* I'm not interested in that. It's dangerous. You know, we make no pretense of being the average Tom, Dick, or Harry—we make no pretense of living in a small cottage or of trying to make our child into an average child, because he can't possibly be an average child, being the son of famous parents. I tried that game with my son Julian, sending him to a comprehensive working-class school, mixing with the people, but the people spat and shit on him because he was famous, as people are wont to do. So his mother had to finally turn around and tell me to piss off: 'I'm sending him to a private school, the kid is suffering here.' "

John now thumbed through *Playboy*. "Take a look at these tits in the front half of the magazine," he said, as he generously shared the issue with me. "They're beautiful. They're not allowed to show pussy, only breasts. Before the Christians got there, the Japanese were absolutely free sexually, like the Tahitians—not in an immoral way, it was natural to them." "And it's the Christians that changed that?" I asked. "Yeh," John replied, "the Christians don't let you have cock and balls. It's the *Judeo*-Christians, just to get *you* in it, too." "You're right," I confessed, "it's all my fault!" "Never mind, never mind," John said, patting me on the shoulder. "But we'd better get on with this since you've only got until Monday. Ask away!"

* * *

It's interesting that no rock-'n'-roll star I can think of has made an album with his wife or whomever and given her fifty percent of the disc.

It's the first time we've done it this way. I know we've made albums together before, like *Live Peace in Toronto 1969* where I had one side and Yoko had the other. And we tried it with the Plastic Ono Band, but there we did it on two separate albums, although we had two similar photos on the covers. But mine, which I call my "Mother" album because it had the song "Mother" on it, got more talked about than hers, and hers went by the wayside, though a lot of people have gotten hip to it now. But *Double Fantasy* is a dialogue, and we have resurrected ourselves, in a way, as John and Yoko—not as John ex-Beatle and Yoko and the Plastic Ono Band. It's just the two of us, and our position was that if the record didn't sell, it meant people didn't want to know about John and Yoko—either they didn't want John anymore or they didn't want John with Yoko or maybe they just wanted Yoko, or whatever. But if they didn't want the two of us, we weren't interested. And this is just the beginning for us. Throughout my career, I've selected to work with—for more than a one-night stand, say, with David Bowie or Elton John—only two people: Paul McCartney and Yoko Ono. O.K.? I brought Paul into the original group, the Quarrymen; he brought George in and George brought Ringo in. I had a say in whether they did join or not, but the only initial move I ever made was bringing Paul McCartney into the group. And the second person who interested me that much as an artist and somebody I could work with was Yoko Ono. That ain't bad picking.

Right now, the public is our only criterion: you can aim for a small public, a medium public, but for meself, I like a large public. And I made my decision in art school, if I'm going to be an artist of whatever description, I want the maximum exposure, not just paint your little pictures in the attic and don't show them to anybody. Otherwise, paint your little pictures in the attic and don't show to anybody, O.K.?

When I arrived in art school, there were lots of artsy-fartsy guys and girls, mainly guys, going round with paint on their jeans and looking just like artists. And they all had lots to talk about and knew all about every damn paintbrush, and they talked about aesthetics, but they all ended up being art teachers or Sunday painters. I got nothing from art school except for a lot of women, a lot of drink, and the freedom to be at college and have fun. I enjoyed it like hell, but for art, I never learned a damn thing.

You've always had a unique, playful drawing style—just think of your book **In His Own Write** *or the album cover and inner sleeve of* **Walls and Bridges** *or your immediately identifiable "Lennonesque" cartoons.*

I did the *Walls and Bridges* drawings when I was ten or eleven. But I found at art school that they tried to knock it out of me, they tried to stop me from drawing how I draw naturally, which I wouldn't let them do. But I never developed it further than cartoons. Somebody once said that cartoonists are people with a good creative gift who are scared of failure as painters, so they make it comedic. My cartoons, to me, are like Japanese brush paintings—if you can't get it in one line, rip it up. Yoko got me into that notion a little when we met, and when she saw that I drew, she'd say, "That's how they do it in Japan, you don't have to make changes . . . *this is it!*"

Yoko and I come from different kinds of backgrounds, but basically we both need this communication. I'm not interested in small, elite groups following or kowtowing to me. I'm interested in communicating whatever it is I want to say or produce in the maximum possible way, and rock 'n' roll is it, as far as I'm concerned. So whether I'm working with Paul or Yoko or Bowie or Elton, it's all toward the same end, whatever that is—self-expression, communication, or just being like a tree, flowering and withering and flowering and withering. So I can never get into the battle of "this album as opposed to that album, this song as opposed to that song, this rose as opposed to that tulip as opposed to that daisy." It's irrelevant.

They say that when one flower opens, many open at the same time, and it's spring everywhere.

That's right.

On Yoko's song "Hard Times Are Over" there seems to be what sounds like a gospel group singing behind Yoko's voice.

There *is* a gospel group singing on it [the Benny Cummings Singers and the Kings Temple Choir]. They were beautiful. Just before the take, they suddenly all took one another's hands and started praying, and Yoko was really crying, and I was emotional because it's right up our alley—whether it's Jesus or Buddha, for us it's all right, either one will do, any of them are all right by us. So there they were, holding hands before the take, and they were singing "Thank you, Jesus, thank you, Lord," and I was like, "Put the tape on! Are you getting this?" And that's what you hear, exactly as it happened—"Thank you, Jesus, thank you, Lord"—and then they go right into the song.

At the end of the session, they thanked God, they thanked our co-producer Jack Douglas, they thanked us for bringing them the work, and we thanked them. And it was the nearest I've ever been to a gospel church service—Phil Spector used to tell me about them, and I always wanted to go and experience it but I was too scared to go. And that was the nearest I've ever been, and it was just beautiful.

It was a working day, with the pressure on—get in the studio and get out—and all the children were there, kids and food and cookies and singing and "Praise the Lord." It was glorious. Putting the gospel choir on that song was a highlight of the session.

On Double Fantasy, *I noticed a mysterious and magical little sound collage that segues between your song "Watching the*

Wheels" and Yoko's charming, thirties-like "Yes, I'm Your
Angel." One hears what seem to be a hawker's voice, the
sounds of a horse-drawn carriage, then a door slamming and
a few musical phrases played by a piano and violin in a res-
taurant.

I'll tell you what it is. One of the voices is me going, "God
bless you, man, thank you, man, cross my palm with silver,
you've got a lucky face," which is what the English guys
who beg or want a tip say, and that's what you hear me
mumbling. And then we re-created the sounds of what
Yoko and I call the Strawberries and Violin Room—the
Palm Court at the Plaza Hotel. We like to sit there occasionally and listen to the old violin and have a cup of tea
and some strawberries. It's romantic. And so the picture is:
There's this kind of street prophet, Hyde Park corner–type
guy who just watches the wheels going around. And
people are throwing money in the hat—we faked that in
the studio, we had friends of ours walking up and down
dropping coins in a hat—and he's saying, Thank you,
thank you, and then you get in the horse carriage and
you go around New York and go into the hotel and the
violins are playing and then this woman comes on and
sings about being an angel.

In "Yes, I'm Your Angel," Yoko sings that she's in your pocket
and that you're in her locket, and the song then segues into

"Woman," which sounds a bit like a troubadour poem written to a medieval lady.

"Woman" came about because, one sunny afternoon in Bermuda, it suddenly hit me what women do for us. Not just what my Yoko does for me, although I was thinking in those personal terms . . . but any truth is universal. What dawned on me was all the games and tricks—never mind the history and the chauvinism and all the things feminists talk about, but everything that I was taking for granted, because that's the way we were brought up. Women really *are* the other half of the sky, as I whisper at the beginning of the song. It's a "we" or it ain't anything. The song came as it was, I didn't try to make it artsy-fartsy or clever, and it reminds me of a Beatles track—I call it the "Beatle John" thing—though I wasn't trying to make it sound like a Beatles track. I did it as I did "Girl" many years ago—it just sort of hit me like a flood, and it came out like that. "Woman" is the grownup version of "Girl."

I know that Yoko is deeply interested in ancient Egyptian art and antiques, and that you have a small collection of it in your home. Regarding "the other half of the sky," it's interesting that in ancient Egyptian mythology, the sky was personified as the goddess Nut—she wasn't Mother Earth—and the earth was personified as the god Neb. And in fact in your song "Yer Blues," you say "My mother was of the sky / My father was of the earth."

185

But I *do* call Yoko "Mother," like our president-elect [Ronald Reagan] calls his wife "Mommy." And for those childless people who find that peculiar, it's because, in general, when you have a child around the house, you tend to refer to each other that way. Yoko calls me "Daddy"—it could be Freudian but it could also mean that Sean refers to me as "Daddy." Occasionally I call her "Mother," because I used to call her "Mother Superior"—if you check your Beatles Fab Four fucking records, "Happiness Is a Warm Gun." She is Mother Superior, she's Mother Earth, she's the mother of my child, she's my mother, she's my daughter . . . the relationship goes through many levels, like most relationships. But it doesn't have any deep-seated strangeness about it.

People are always judging or criticizing you, or focusing on what you're trying to say on one little album, on one little song, but to me it's a lifetime's work. From the boyhood paintings and poetry to when I die—it's all part of one big production. And I don't have to announce that this album is part of a larger work: if it isn't obvious, then forget it. But I did put a little clue on the beginning of *Double Fantasy*—the bells on "(Just Like) Starting Over." The head of the album is a wishing bell of Yoko's. And it's like the beginning of "Mother" on my Plastic Ono album, which had a very slow death bell. So it's taken a long time to get from that slow church death bell to this sweet little wishing bell. And that's the connection. To me, my work is one piece.

In "Woman," you also sing about how Yoko allowed you to express your inner feelings, and then thanked her "for showing me the meaning of success."

I'm not saying success as a famous artist and star is no good, and I'm not saying it's great. The thing about the "Working Class Hero" song that nobody ever got right was that it was supposed to be sardonic. It had nothing to do with socialism, it had to do with "If you want to go through that trip, you'll get up to where I am, and this is what you'll be—some guy whining on a record, all right? If you want to do it, do it." Because I've been successful as an artist and have been happy and unhappy, and I've been unknown in Liverpool or Hamburg and been happy and unhappy. But what Yoko's taught me is what the *real* success is—the success of my personality, the success of my relationship with her and the child, my relationship with the world . . . and to be happy when I wake up. It has nothing to do with rock machinery or *not* rock machinery.

What am I supposed to be, some kind of martyr that's not supposed to be rich? Did they criticize me when I was a Beatle for making money? In retrospect, a lot of money came our way, and I spent a lot of it, I sure as hell had a lot of fun with it, I didn't throw it all away—what about the psychedelic Rolls-Royce? But through ignorance, I lost a lot of it and gave a lot of it away through maybe a misplaced charitable heart, I don't know. So why are they suddenly attacking me for making money now? Because we were associated with radical causes, feminism, and the antiwar movement. To be antiwar you have to be poor? There's many a socialist in the House of Lords, what are they talking about? I mean, if they want a poor man, they can follow Jesus. And he's not only poor, he's dead!

Some asshole recently wrote a cover story about me in *Esquire*. [Journalist Laurence Shames's virulent article "John Lennon, Where Are You?" appeared in the November 1980 issue. In it, Shames wrote: "I was looking for the Lennon who had always shot his mouth off, who had offended everyone without having to try. My Lennon was a bitter clown, a man of extravagant error and vast resilience, a big baby, an often pathetic truth-seeker whose pained, goofy, earnest, and paranoid visage was the emblem and conscience of his age. . . . The Lennon I would have found is a forty-year-old businessman who watches a lot of television, who's got $150 million, a son he dotes on, and a wife who intercepts his phone calls . . . Is it true, John? Have you really given up?"] This guy spent twenty months chasing cows and gardeners and deeds. I'm busy making a record, and that asshole's looking at cows. For fuck's sake, man, what are they talking about? What should I have bought—slaves? Hookers? [*Laughing*] They've got minds like fucking sewers to sell magazines, to sell products that people can't afford to buy, that they don't need and have to replace every three months . . . and they're accusing me of what? That guy is the kind of person who used to be in love with you and now hates you—a rejected lover. I don't even know the asshole, but he was chasing an illusion, fell out of love with it, and now hates another illusion. Neither one of the people he's describing ever existed, it's only in his head. It had nothing to do with me—it could be Greta Garbo he's talking about, right?

These critics with the illusions they've created about artists—it's like idol worship. Like those little kids in Liverpool who only liked us when we were in Liverpool; a lot of them dropped us because we got big in Manchester, right? They thought we'd sold out. Then the English got upset because we got big in . . . What the hell is it? They only like people when they're on the way up, and when they're up there, they've got nothing else to do but shit on them. They like to imagine they create and break people, but they don't. I cannot be on the way up again, and I cannot be twenty-five again. I cannot be what I was five minutes ago, so I can't waste the time on considering what they're going to say or what they're going to do. Most of them are now half my age and know shit from Shinola about anything other than from 1970 on. What they want is dead heroes, like Sid Vicious and James Dean. I'm not interested in being a dead fucking hero . . . So forget 'em, forget 'em.

You know what Eugene O'Neill said about critics? "I love every bone in their heads." You see, the only way

189

to deal with critics is to go *over* their heads *direct* to the public. That's what we did with the Bed-Ins and with our *Two Virgins* and Plastic Ono albums, and that's what we're doing now. The record is already a success, it doesn't matter a damn what anybody writes about it. And we hear from all kinds of people—some letters are addressed just to me, some are addressed just to Yoko, and the majority are addressed to both of us. We got one letter from a five-year-old who lives in Australia—that's the bit I get emotional about, that's the bit that affects me. And I also get affected by the letters we receive from Brazil or Poland or Austria, places that I'm not conscious of in my mind. One kid living up in Yorkshire wrote this heartfelt letter about being both Oriental and English and identifying with John and Yoko. The odd kid in the class. There are a lot of those kids who identify with us—as a couple, a biracial couple, who stand for love, peace, feminism, and the positive things of the world. They're the ones we're talking to.

But the press are always looking at the neck of the giraffe as it goes past the window—that's how the game goes. So there's absolutely no way they can ever keep up. And does anybody ever look at the writing of these critics? You'd think nothing had happened in writing—no William Burroughs, no Ginsberg, no Dylan, no *nothing* if you look at the way these people write. They're criticizing us for what we're doing and how we're doing it, and they do so in schoolboy-essay style with three-syllable words.

Most of the petty resentment is mainly from the sixties rock critics who are reaching that age where the beer belly is getting larger. The younger ones are into the new wave, and some of the older ones are trying to get into it, but they don't really appreciate it, they'd just as soon be listening to *Sgt. Pepper* and *Exile on Main Street* and *Highway 61 Revisited* or whatever it was. And the sixties rock critics are locked into the sixties more than they'd like to admit, and they're becoming our parents . . . and the artist's job is *not* to get locked into *any* period, whether it's the sixties, the seventies, or the eighties. Most of those critics haven't got the guts of someone like Jon Landau [music critic, record producer, and Bruce Springsteen's manager] to get out there and *do* it. I admire Lester Bangs, who's a musician as well as a critic, and I'm sure there's many times he shit all over me, and I'm sure Landau must have, in his time, both praised and hated me. I've had it both ways from all the major critics. But at least some of them *do it*. And as I said in "Lennon Remembers," and as I said in art school, I'm a *doer*, not a voyeur . . . And I've got nothing to hide. Remember the song?

"Everybody's Got Something to Hide Except Me and My Monkey," where you sing about your inside being out and your outside being in, and your outside being in and your inside being out.

Right, but what did the critics say? "A bit simplistic, no imagery in it." Perhaps I should have said: "Your inside is like a whale juice dripping from the fermented foam of the teenyboppers' VD in Times Square as I injected my white clown face with heroin and performed in red-leather knickers." Maybe then they'd like it, right?

That's great, that sounds like Allen Ginsberg.

Right, we can all do Ginsberg—and I like Ginsberg. But try shaving it all off and getting down to the nitty-gritty—that's what I always tried to write, except for the occasional "Walrus" bit. I'm not interested in describing a fucking tree. I'm interested in climbing it or being under it.

"No one I think is in my tree."

Yeh, well, that was imagery. Because I was more self-conscious then and paranoid. It was that bit about not knowing "Am I crazy or what?" The eternal questions.

All the way through your work, there's this incredibly strong notion about inspiring people to be themselves and to come together to try to change things. I'm thinking here, obviously, of songs like "Give Peace a Chance," "Power to the People," and "Happy Xmas (War Is Over)."

It's still there. If you look on the vinyl around the new record's logo [on the twelve-inch single "(Just Like) Starting Over"]—which all the kids have done already all over the world from Brazil to Australia to Poland—inside is written: ONE WORLD, ONE PEOPLE. So we continue. "Give Peace a Chance," not "Shoot People for Peace." "All You Need Is Love": it's damn hard, but I absolutely believe it.

We all want war to go away, but you can't just sit around waiting for it to happen. It's like what they said after the Holocaust. "First they came for the Jews and I did not speak out because I was not a Jew. Then they came for me, and there was no one left to speak out for me." It's that same thing today, only not such a pressured, horrific scene. But you first have to be *conscious* and imagine there's no countries, not "This is the answer to the universe, let's get rid of the passports tomorrow."

First of all, *conceive* of the idea of no nation, no passport. If you're not defending a nation there's nothing to fight about. We've said it a million times—first of all we conceived of flying, then we flew. It took a long time to get up in the air, and it was a lot of sticking feathers together and melting under the sun and all that, but conceiving the idea is the first move.

We're not the first to say "Imagine No Countries" or "Give Peace a Chance," but we're carrying that torch, like the Olympic torch, passing it hand to hand, to each other,

193

to each country, to each generation . . . and that's our job. Not to live according to somebody else's idea of how we should live—rich, poor, happy, not happy, smiling, not smiling, wearing the right jeans, not wearing the right jeans.

I'm not claiming divinity, I've never claimed purity of soul, I've never claimed to have the answers to life. I only put out songs and answer questions as honestly as I can, but *only* as honestly as I can—no more, no less. I cannot live up to other people's expectations of me because they're illusionary. I cannot be a punk in Hamburg and Liverpool, because I'm older now. I see the world through different eyes now. But I still believe in peace, love, and understanding, as Elvis Costello said. What's so fucking funny about peace, love, and understanding? It's fashionable to be a go-getter and slash thy neighbor with a cross, but we're not one to follow the fashion.

It's like your song "The Word."

Yes, the word was "love."

"Why in the world are we here? / Surely not to live in pain and fear"—that's from "Instant Karma!" And that's an idea in all of your and Yoko's work . . . as when she tells us in her new song "Beautiful Boys" that we should never be afraid to cry or be afraid to be afraid. I found that beautiful.

That is beautiful. I'm often afraid, but I'm not afraid to be afraid, though it's always scary.

When Yoko sings "Hard times are over," she adds: "for a while." She doesn't say they're over forever.

No, no. She knows better. [*Laughing*] But at least when it's all right, let's enjoy it! What's more painful is to try *not* to be yourself. People spend a lot of time trying to be somebody else, and I think it leads to terrible diseases. Maybe you get cancer or something. A lot of tough guys die of cancer, have you noticed? John Wayne, Steve McQueen. I think it has something to do—I don't know, I'm not an expert—with constantly living or getting trapped in an image or an illusion of themselves, suppressing some part of themselves, whether it's the feminine side or the fearful side.

I once heard some Blue Meanie–type of person say, "You know, that John Lennon really has a super-enlarged sense of himself."

Explain.

I think that he was referring to a comment you once made to the effect that sometimes you thought you were a loser and other times that you were God almighty.

Well, we all think that, don't we? Everybody goes through that. When something is put down in print, it looks like it's being writ by Moses on the tablets. One has to deal with the reality that when it comes out of your mouth and it goes into print—and after years and years of answering the same questions, basically, over and over again—one tends to get it down into the simplest form, and the simplest form is that we all feel almighty some days and we all feel no-mighty other days, and that's all that's saying. Sometimes you look in the mirror and "Oh, isn't it wonderful?" And other times "What is *that*, I hate it!" I don't know anybody who isn't like that. Sometimes you love yourself, sometimes you hate yourself, and as I believe that we all contain God and we are all God, so the fact that I think I'm God almighty some days is fine, because I think we're *all* God almighty. I'll compare myself with any creature, living or dead, the potential's in me just as it's in any one of us to be God or the devil, Picasso or Norman Rockwell or the *Peanuts* artist Charles Schulz.

In "Instant Karma!" you ask us if we really think that we're superstars, and then you inform us that that's exactly *who we are.*

Of course, of course.

These songs really answer those questions.

Yeh, it's all in the songs, but people just forget the song that came before. It's the giraffe going past the window again.

In your new song "Watching the Wheels," you sing, "People asking questions lost in confusion / Well I tell them there's no problem, only solutions." But there are some people who don't put that much stock in solutions.

Well, that's their problem. I haven't perfected the art of life—I'm learning, but I'll probably go to the grave learning it. If one just spends time concentrating on a problem, that's all you do. But if one puts one's mind on the solution, the problem tends to go away. I've found this out by trial and error, and I can't do it on call like [*snaps his fingers*]. But what I'm saying in this song is: I've found this out, what do *you* think, folks? So I'm just answering the questions that people have been asking me in the letters I've been receiving during the past five years. If we had answered the questions by making a movie called *Love Story*, with Ryan O'Neal acting John and Ali MacGraw acting Yoko—or called it *Fred and Ada* and dressed in clown suits—would that have been more acceptable? Maybe, but it's not our style. We are the people who did the Bed-Ins for Peace, which was our Living Theater, and our life is our art.

I notice that in nearly every interview you've done, you're continually asked, "What do you think of Paul, George, and Ringo?"

Right. Journalists used to ask me to tell them the story of how I wrote "Strawberry Fields," and I used to say, "O.K., I was making the film *How I Won the War* in Almería in Spain, the Beatles had just stopped touring, I was going through this trauma, and then when we got in the studio I didn't like Paul's attitude." But that was *then*, I'm not telling that *now*. I just saw Ringo two days ago, and I can tell you hundreds of things I might have been mad at him about when something happened in the past, but I'm not carrying any cross. It's the press that wants to know about the fucking Beatles. You ask me about the Beatles, I'll tell you what I feel about them. But if you look in the new *Playboy* interview I did a couple of months ago, *carefully*, you'll see that I said, "I love those guys, I love the Beatles, I'm proud of the music, I admire a lot of what Paul's done since we split up, I think a lot of it's shit." What do they want from me? So maybe it was sibling rivalry then. Maybe it's still in my subconscious—who gives a shit? Paul doesn't really give a shit. George doesn't really give a shit, and Ringo doesn't really give a shit. It's *you* assholes always talking about it—I don't mean *you* personally. Do you understand? Do you understand what the game is? The press come up, ask us about each other just to get some quote to go back and sell newspapers with, and then tell us we're a lot of rich farts bitching about each other.

O.K., let's get back to reality for a moment. And speaking of reality, there's another aspect of your work, which has to do with the way you continually question what's real and what's illusory, such as in "Look at Me," your new "Watching the Wheels," and, of course, "Strawberry Fields Forever," in which you sing, "Nothing is real."

In a way, *no thing* is real, if you break the word down. As the Hindus or Buddhists say, it's an illusion. It's *Rashomon.* We all see it, but the agreed-upon illusion is what we live in. And the hardest thing is facing yourself. It's easier to shout "Revolution" and "Power to the People" than it is to look at yourself and try and find out what's real inside you and what isn't, when you pull the wool over your own eyes, your own hypocrisy. That's the hardest.

I used to think that the world was doing it to me and the world owed me something, and that either the conservatives or the socialists or the fascists or the communists or the Christians or the Jews were doing something to me. And when you're a teenybopper, that's what you think. But I'm forty now, and I don't think that anymore, 'cause I found out it doesn't fucking work! The thing goes on anyway, and all you're doing is jacking off, screaming what your mommy or daddy did . . . but one has to go through that. For the people who even bother to go through that—most assholes just accept what is and get on with it, right? But for the few of us who did question what was going on . . . well, I've found out for me personally—*not* for the whole world—that I am responsible for me, as *well* as for them. I am part of them. There's no separation: We're all one, right? So in that respect I look at it all and think, "Ah, I have to deal with me again in that way. What is real? What is the illusion I'm living or not living?" And I have to deal with it every day. The layers of the onion.

"Looking through a glass onion."

That's what it's about, isn't it?

Yoko came in to say that she and John had to leave for the Record Plant—the legendary, now defunct recording studio on West Forty-fourth Street where albums like Jimi Hendrix's *Electric Ladyland* and Bruce Springsteen's *Born to Run* were recorded, and where, for the past couple of weeks, John and Yoko have been remixing some of Yoko's old songs and putting finishing touches on her new single, "Walking on Thin Ice." They would be working there throughout the night . . . and why didn't I join them? It was around ten p.m. when we left the Dakota and got into the waiting car. Arriving at the Record Plant half an hour later, we entered the main studio and were immediately greeted by a sonic blast whose force almost sent me reeling backward, as out of the speakers came the shattering cascade of the accelerated high-energy vocal particles of Yoko's inimitable, primordial voice—intersected by John's forward and backward guitar tracks—screaming out for us to open our boxes, our trousers, our thighs, our legs, our ears, our noses. And over the next six hours, and as two sound engineers and producer Jack Douglas (who co-produced *Double Fantasy* with John and Yoko) remixed a number of Yoko's songs ("Open Your Box," "Kiss Kiss Kiss," "Every Man Has a Woman Who Loves Him"), John and I continued our conversation until four in the morning.

* * *

Is Yoko thinking of putting out a disco album?

I can't really verify what we're doing yet, because with Yoko, you never know until it's done. But we did come in here to make this string of songs that might go to the rock and disco clubs.

And what about your new songs?

No, because I don't make that stuff. [*Laughing*] I mean, what way could I have come back into this game? I came back from where I know best, as unpretentious as possible . . . and with no experimentation, because I was happy to be doing it as I did it before. My song "Starting Over"—I call it "Elvis-Orbison": "Only the lonely know why I cry / Only the lonely."

All the musicians—and I gather there were about twenty of them—sound great on the new album.

That's because we had a good time. Because they get bored with doing clever little jazz riffs. When I give them some straight rock, they love it. You could see it in their faces when they were doing "Starting Over," which is the simplest of the songs in a way . . . that's when they all said, "When are we going on tour?"

There's a bit of slap-back echo on your recording.

Well, the tape echo is from the fifties. A lot of the records I made had the same echo on them . . . all the way back to "Rock and Roll Music." I love it. And my voice has always sounded pretty much the same. I'm going right back to the roots of my past. It's like Dylan doing *Nashville Skyline*. But I don't have any Nashville, being from Liverpool, so I go back to the records I knew, which is Elvis and Roy Orbison and Gene Vincent and Jerry Lee Lewis. If I felt like making one, I could make a disco record, I could make a waltz, I could make a country record, but my interests happen to lie in fifties rock 'n' roll and blues. "I'm Losing You" is a kind of blues. It's just the style of the song, it's like a watercolor as opposed to oil. I like to dabble. And I occasionally get tripped off into a "Revolution 9," but my far-out side has been completely encompassed by Yoko.

You know, the first show we did together was at Cambridge University in 1969, when she had been booked to do a concert with some jazz musicians. That was the first time I had appeared un-Beatled. I just had an amp and I played feedback, and she howled and screamed, and people got very upset because they recognized me: "What's *he* doing with you?" It's always: "Stay in your bag." So when she tried to rock, they said, "What's *she* doing here?" And when I went with her and tried to be the instrument and not project—to just be her band, like a sort of Ike Turner to her Tina, only her Tina was a different, avant-garde Tina—well, even some of the jazz guys got upset.

Everybody has pictures they want you to live up to. But that's the same as living up to your parents' expectations, or to society's expectations, or to so-called critics who are just guys with a pen or a typewriter in a little room, smoking and drinking beer and having their dreams and nightmares, too, and getting paid once a week or once a month, watching TV and buying records and doing what everybody else is doing, but somehow pretending that they're living in a different, separate world. That's all right, that's what they have to do. But there are people who break out of their bags.

I remember years ago when you and Yoko appeared in bags at a Vienna press conference.

Right. We sang a Japanese folk song in the bags. "Das ist really you, John? John Lennon in zee bag?" Yeh, it's me. "But how do we know ist you?" Because I'm telling you. "Vy don't you come out from this bag?" Because I don't want to come out of the bag. "Don't you realize this is the Hapsburg Palace?" I thought it was a hotel. "Vell, it is now a hotel." They had great chocolate cake in that Viennese hotel, I remember that. Anyway, who wants to be locked in a bag? You have to break out of your bag to keep alive.

You guys really have quite a sense of humor.

Of course we have a sense of humor. Anyone who can get in a bag and do an interview with the Austrian press *has* to have a sense of humor!
    [The studio engineers are now playing a tape of Yoko's new song, "Walking on Thin Ice."]
    Listen to this, Jonathan. We were thinking that this song is so damn good that she should put her own single out, independently, with me on the B side. I'd love to be on the B side of a hit record after all these years. I'd settle for

it any day. Yoko deserves it, it's been a long haul. Me just being the guitarist—I'm playing backwards guitar on this song.

Listening to it, I actually can't distinguish your guitar from her voice.

Right. If you listen to the song "Why" on Yoko's first Plastic Ono album, it's just my guitar and her voice—you don't know the difference. That was the first session we did together, and I was just letting loose, trying to follow her, and when we heard it back, we didn't know which was which, either. It's incredible. Fucking great! And as I said, Yoko deserves her own single. I wouldn't fight about it at all.

And speaking of fighting—and this will make you laugh—Andy Warhol once wanted Yoko and me to wrestle at Madison Square Garden, and he'd film it!

You must be kidding. He wanted you two to wrestle? Maybe a sumo contest!

Anything. Just to show the great "peace and love" people having a good fight onstage—it might have been great!

Do you and Yoko have any plans now, not to fight in public but maybe to tour together?

I don't know. We've got plenty of plans, and we have talked about touring. But as usual, as soon as I say I'm going to tour, I get nervous because everybody keeps asking, "So when are you going on tour?" And then I don't want to do it. And if I announce that I'm not going on tour, then I immediately want to tour. But it might be fun. Can you imagine the two of us now with these new songs . . . and if we did some of Yoko's early stuff, like "Don't Worry, Kyoko" or "Open Your Box" or "Why" from her Plastic Ono album—it's just her voice and my guitar and one bass and drums, and I hear all those licks coming out now from some of today's groups. So we just might do it. But there will be no smoke bombs, no lipstick, no flashing lights. It has to be just comfy. But we could have a laugh. We're born-again rockers, and we're starting over.

And you could also have your own late-night TV show . . . like The Captain and Tennille. [*Pop music artists "Captain" Daryl Dragon and Toni Tennille had an ABC variety series in the late seventies.*]

Yeh, of course we could. John and Yoko might do it one day . . . but I haven't got any plans so don't get excited! But being me, being John and Yoko, where would we go for maximum exposure? Maybe from our bed: "And now live from John and Yoko's bedroom!" [*Laughing*] We often talk about that. It might be fun. But there's time, right? Plenty of time. Right now here we are in the Record Plant, talking to Jonathan Cott again for *Rolling Stone* . . . and it will be fun to be on the cover of *Rolling Stone*. It will be fun, won't it, to start 1981 like 1968?

"Look out kid / You're doin' it again."

Right. And who's going to be the first to go—Lennon or *Rolling Stone*? Who do you think's going to be around the longest? *Life, Time, Newsweek, Playboy, Look, Rolling Stone*? Let's face it, magazines come and go, record executives come and go, record companies come and go, film producers come and go. Artists come and go, too. What a life!

You know, the last album I did before *Double Fantasy* was *Rock 'n' Roll*, with the cover picture of me in Hamburg in a leather jacket. At the end of making that record, I was finishing up a track that Phil Spector had made me sing called "Just Because," which I really didn't know—all the rest of the songs I'd done as a teenager, so I knew them backwards—and I couldn't get the hang of it. At the end of that record—I was mixing it just next door—I started spieling and saying, "And so we say farewell from the Record Plant," and a little thing in the back of my mind said, "Are you *really* saying farewell?" I hadn't thought of it then. I was still separated from Yoko and still hadn't had the baby, but somewhere in the back was a voice that was saying, "Are you saying farewell to the whole game?"

It just flashed by like that—like a premonition. I didn't think of it until a few years later, when I realized that I had actually stopped recording. I came across the cover photo—the original picture of me in my leather jacket, leaning against the wall in Hamburg in 1961—andI thought, "Is this it? Do I start where I came in, with 'Be-Bop-A-Lula'?" The day I first met Paul I was singing that song for the first time onstage. There's a photo in all the Beatles books—a picture of me with a checked shirt on, holding a little acoustic guitar—and I'm singing "Be-Bop-A-Lula," just as I did on that album.

It was like this little thing, and there was no consciousness in it. It was only much later, when I started thinking about it . . . you know, like sometimes you dream—it's like a premonition, but this was an awake premonition. I had no plans, no intention, but I thought, "What is this, this cover photo from Hamburg, this 'Be-Bop-A-Lula,' this saying goodbye from the Record Plant?" And I was actually *really* saying goodbye since it was the last track of the *Rock 'n' Roll* album—and I was so glad to get it over with and it was also the end of the album.

It's like when a guy in England, an astrologer, once told me that I was going to *not* live in England. And I didn't remember that until I was in the middle of my immigration fight to stay in this country and when I thought, "What the hell am I doing here? Why the hell am I going through this?" I didn't plan to live here, it just happened. There was no packing the bags—we left everything at our house in England, we were just coming for a short visit . . . but we never went back.

I was in court, and people were saying I wasn't good enough to be here or that I was a communist or whatever the hell it was. So I thought, "What am I doing this for?" And then I remembered that astrologer in London telling me, "One day you'll live abroad." Not because of taxes. The story was that I left for tax reasons, but I didn't, I got no benefit, nothing, I screwed up completely, I lost money when I left. So I had no reason to leave England. I'm not a person who looks for the sun like a lot of the English who like to get away to the south of France, or go to Malta or Spain or Portugal. George was always talking about, "Let's all go and live in the sun."

"Here Comes the Sun."

Right, he's always looking for the sun because he's still living in England . . . And then it clicked on me, "Jesus, that guy *predicted* I was going to leave England!" Though at the time he said that to me, I was thinking, "Are you kidding?"

Sometimes you wonder, I mean really wonder. I know we make our own reality and we always have a choice, but how much is preordained? Is there always a fork in the road and are there two preordained paths that are equally preordained? There could be hundreds of paths where one could go this way or that way—there's a choice, and it's very strange sometimes.

And that's a good ending for our interview.

t was now four o'clock in the morning. The album's co-producer, Jack Douglas, was still sitting in front of the control board and remixing a couple of Yoko's songs; Yoko was napping on a studio couch; and John was talking to me about how happy he felt being able to live in New York City where, unlike in England or Japan, he could raise his son without racial prejudice; of his memory of the first rock-'n'-roll song he ever wrote, a takeoff on the Del-Vikings' "Come Go with Me," in which he changed the lines to "Come come come come / Come and go with me / To the peni-peni-tentiary"; and of some of the things he had learned on his many trips around the world during the past five years. As he walked me to the elevator, I mentioned to him how exhilarating it was to see Yoko and him looking and sounding so well. "I love her, and we're together," he said. "Goodbye, till next time."

CODA

"I have a story to tell you," Yoko said when I met up with her at Stockholm's regal Grand Hotel and joined her for breakfast at the Veranda restaurant that overlooks the city's waterfront, the Old Town, and the Royal Palace. Dressed that morning in matching black jacket and trousers, and wearing a black trilby hat and dark-tinted glasses, she had come to Stockholm for several days in mid-March to oversee preparations for an exhibition of her work that would be opening in June at the Moderna Museet and that would include a selection of the koan-like instruction pieces from her book *Grapefruit* that are as heart- and mind-awakening today as they were when she had begun imagining and creating them more than fifty years ago.

As indefatigable as ever—I was flabbergasted when I realized that she would be turning eighty on February 18, 2013—Yoko had two weeks earlier traveled to Vienna to receive the prestigious 2012 Oskar Kokoschka Prize, Austria's highest award for applied contemporary art. She was at that moment in the midst of a two-month whirlwind tour of Europe that was taking her not only to Vienna and Stockholm but also to Copenhagen, Berlin, Reykjavik, and then on to London where she was preparing a major retrospective of her work at the Serpentine Gallery, for which Yoko would be inviting people to upload and send their smiles by mobile phone and online to create a global anthology of beaming portraits. In spite of her crushing schedule, Yoko and I had recently discussed the possibility of getting together to do an interview; and as I had been planning for a while to visit some friends in Sweden, and as Yoko thought that since she might be able to find some free time during the three days that she'd be staying in Stockholm, she suggested that this might be the perfect place and the opportune moment for us to meet up and chat about days past, present, and future.

Yoko ordered fried eggs and tea, and then said, "The story I wanted to tell you is about my first meeting with John. It was when I was having my first show in London at the Indica Gallery. I don't know how that happened—it was incredible, but everything has some meaning. John had just come to the gallery directly from 3 Abbey Road—that's the address of Abbey Road Studios—and the number 3 in numerology stands for music. And I was at number 6 Masons Yard, which was the address of the Indica Gallery—and the number 6 stands for love. So on that very day music came to love."

Music introduced itself to love that day—November 8, 1966—but it was only two years later, on May 19, 1968, that John and Yoko—the Two Virgins—spent their first night together making music and then making love. Twelve years later in 1980 they recorded and released their album *Double Fantasy* on which Yoko sang an insouciant 1930s-type birthday song for John called "Yes, I'm Your Angel" ("Yes, I'm so pretty . . . And we're so happy every day") and made a wish that all his wishes would come true. *Double Fantasy* would turn out to be John and Yoko's final collaboration, completing the full circle of their life together in the same way it had begun, with music and love, which, as the composer Hector Berlioz once remarked, are "the two wings of the soul."

"When I was making preparations to come to see you in Stockholm," I said to Yoko, "I suddenly realized that I've actually known you for forty-four years. I can't believe it."

"Was it that long ago?" she asked me.

"I met you and John when you were both living at Montagu Square in London. That was in September 1968. And when I was recently thinking back on those times, the first thing that struck me was that you really haven't changed at all."

"You don't think so?"

"I mean that your values and commitments and loyalties are still the same. You've really remained true blue and haven't gotten cynical at all. How did you manage to stay yourself?"

"Yes, I'm the same person. I'm *extremely* myself," she said, laughing. "But I hope it doesn't sound as if I mean that in an egotistical sense. I just don't believe in people trying to be *not* themselves. In some religions, people feel it's very bad to be *you*, that you have to give up yourself to God or whatever, but if you don't have yourself, how can *you* give?"

"I read somewhere that you once sent a postcard to John when he was in India that said 'Watch for me—I'm a cloud in the sky!' In fact, you've always seemed to me to have had your head in the clouds, but at the same time you've still always managed to keep your feet on the ground. That's quite an accomplishment."

"Well, that's because head is up and feet are down!" she told me, laughing again. "It's just natural for an animal of our caliber to be like that."

"When I think of all the creative work that you do," I remarked to her, "what strikes me is that it all seems to exemplify what the Zen teacher Shunryu Suzuki calls the beginner's mind. He says, 'If your mind is empty, it's always ready for anything and is open to everything. In the beginner's mind there are many possibilities, in the expert's mind there are few.' "

"Well," she said, "think about going shopping. You go

shopping and then you come home with two enormous bags, and if you're carrying those bags, you can't see where you're going and you just fall down. And the same thing can be said about your head: You're carrying so many things—history, memories, everything society has tried to teach you—and you therefore can't really have your own thoughts in there. In fact, many people don't have *any* thoughts of their own in there. It's much better to just have a clean space in there so that new things can come in. So, yes, I'm a beginner, and I will probably be a better beginner in about two or three years because I'm continually cleaning myself. And here's another thing: My whole life has been a kind of education for me—I'm always learning things—it's all a process of learning, and I still have much more to learn. Every day I recognize new things in my mind. And I think that we're actually just products of our minds. The body is just a product of our mind."

Many years ago, I had read that Picasso, throughout the eighty years that he was doing his creative work starting as a teenager, supposedly completed a painting or some other kind of artwork every seventy-two hours. And it sometimes seemed to me that Yoko was giving Picasso a run for his money. Her book *YES YOKO ONO*, which is an exhaustive overview of her artistic career between the years 1961 and 2000, lists more than 750 of her art and photography exhibitions, performance events, concerts, films, and recordings; and one should remember that between the years 1975 and

1980, when she and John took their five-year "sabbatical," Yoko created no new music or artworks of any kind. During the past thirteen years, however, she has made up for lost time. In my final interview with John in December 1980, he told me: "Yoko never stops. You come into the house and there's four hundred poems and ideas ... she's absolutely incredible—she's selling a cow with one hand and writing a poem with the other." And in an e-mail that Yoko sent me in 2010, she stated: "I write to keep myself from jumping off the sky, and I do it at the speed of an electric typewriter. Writing is my security blanket, as is music and painting." So I decided to ask her how she had managed to accomplish so much and to avoid being stymied by creative blocks.

"I've managed to do that," Yoko told me, "by not holding on to what I've done. For instance, I haven't even *read* that book *YES YOKO ONO,* so I'm not blocked with the memory of all those things. I even have a hard time remembering the lyrics of my songs! It's like what happens to psychics—they say something and then don't remember what they've just said."

"This is certainly a non sequitur, and it may sound strange," I admitted to her, "but I've always wanted to talk to you about your special relationship with the sky. Did you know that in French there's the term *don du ciel*—a gift from the sky? You seem to have received a lot of those gifts."

"Yes, that's beautiful, and I actually have talked about receiving gifts from the sky."

"And it's interesting," I added, "that in French, the word *ciel* means both sky *and* heaven."

"That's bad, though!" she exclaimed.

"In 'Imagine,' John suggests that we should all imagine that there's no heaven, and no hell below us, and above us only sky."

"Yes, that's right!"

"Someone I know recently flew to Liverpool, and he informed me that in 2002 the Liverpool Airport was renamed the Liverpool John Lennon Airport. He said that inside the main building there's a seven-foot-tall bronze statue of John overlooking the check-in hall. And it really blew my mind when I learned that the motto of the airport, which is painted on its roof, is 'Above Us Only Sky.' "

"Yes, they got the message. Did you ever notice that when you're in a plane the vibrations you're feeling that are coming to you are totally different from the ones you feel when you're on the ground? But when you go up there, it's only sky—you're free from all those earthly vibrations. And it's so beautiful. A lot of the things I've written were done up in the sky."

LiverpoolJohn LennonAirport

above us only sky

I recalled that during World War II, Yoko's mother had taken refuge with her three children in a rural Japanese farming village where Yoko, who was constantly teased by the local children, would find comfort simply by lying on her back on a tatami and looking up at the sky through an opening in the roof, later explaining that she used her powers of visualization in order to survive. In her song "Sky People," she proclaimed: "Sky People, that's what we are." In another song, "Silver Horse," she expressed the wish that someone "might take me to that deep blue sky"; and John Lennon, who would eventually take her there, referred to her as "Yoko in the Sky with Diamonds."

Among Yoko's many imaginative sky-themed creations are *Glass Keys to Open the Sky*, which consists of four glass keys in a Plexiglas box; a 2008 installation called *Liverpool Skyladders* in which she positioned some twenty-five stepladders, contributed by members of the public, on the site of Liverpool's roofless, bombed-out St. Luke's Church, hoping that it would enable people "to find space for dreams and the imagination under the open skies"; and her video installation *Sky TV*, which she created in 1966 and which was one of the first examples of video sculpture. Each time that I visit the Asia Society in New York City, I always make it a point to look at this permanent installation in which a video camera, placed on the roof of the building and trained on the sky, feeds real-time images of the sky twenty-four hours a day onto a television monitor located in the museum's lobby.

When someone once remarked about an astronomer that "he knew the sky by heart," he might also have had Yoko in mind.

"Yes," she affirmed to me, "my work really is a kind of wish and a hope for having more and more sky. When you're thirsty you want to drink some chilled water, and so in this sense you want to drink the sky."

"In John's song 'Cold Turkey,'" I reminded Yoko, "he screams out in pain 'Can't see no future / Can't see no sky,' as if not to see the sky is both a cause and a sign of deep depression."

"Yes, I think that the sky really is like a cure."

"But there's another side to this," I mentioned. "One of Emily Dickinson's most beautiful poems begins 'The Brain is wider than the Sky,' and in it she suggests that if you place the brain and the sky next to each other, the brain will contain not only the sky but also everyone else in the world as well. And as if to mirror that sentiment, the Japanese Zen master Muso Soseki said that, for a Zen practitioner, there should be no limits, and declared: 'The blue sky must feel ashamed to be so small!'"

"So that's to say that the conceptual reality is something bigger than the sky," Yoko observed. "And this reminds me that the reason I have so much hope for the human race is because we just haven't brought forth all of our powers yet, and our powers are bigger than the sky. And the fact that this was said by someone in the West, and also by someone

Have you seen the horizon lately?

Y.O.

in the East, just shows that we're together. It's as if Dickinson and Soseki are like cells on one huge body!"

"I'm always moved," I remarked to Yoko, "whenever I think of the way you consoled yourself as a young girl during the war by daydreaming and staring up at the sky. It's been said that giving the brain the freedom to drift and wander enables it to solve problems that most likely can't be solved by just using mobile devices. I remember that when I was young, I used to spend a lot of time daydreaming and just staring out the window and looking at the trees. Today, almost all of the kids I see are just staring at their video games."

"Well, I don't play video games," she said, laughing.

"Have you ever thought of creating your own Yoko Ono video game?" I asked her half jokingly.

"I've sort of thought about doing something like that," she said, "something that would bring people a step up. But, you know, you don't really have to do that because people get to be 'stepped up' anyway. I think that modern technology is like doorknobs—it's sort of inconvenient not to have a doorknob, so we created doorknobs . . . to open the door to the next world."

"To the next world?"

"Yes, the next world."

"In the not-so-long-ago world," I pointed out, "you were the recipient of an astonishing amount of unspeakably racist taunting and other kinds of abuse. How did you ever manage to deal with that?"

"Yes, they really wanted to kill me," she said, "and my unpopularity also made them hate John as well because of me. I guess you could say that we raised some emotions in them."

"You later explained why you were able to live through that time by saying, 'If you're centered and can transform that negative energy, it will help you. If you believe it's going to kill you, it will kill you.' You seem to have somehow been able to turn that hate-energy around and use it to your advantage. Like judo."

"Yes, just like judo. Making use of all that negative power that was being directed to me."

"I remember reading a newspaper article at that time in which a journalist asserted that you were without doubt the most hated woman in the world."

"It's true, I was. But I myself was living in a different world. I thought it was very important for all of us to do our best to keep the world floating and not sinking—and that's what I was trying to do, and I was proud of all the things that I was making. Now, most people don't think that you should be *proud* of what you're making. But we *must* be proud of what we do—to create good music, good art, good films—but also in the sense that a kind of perfection emanates a kind of special vibration, and this perfection always includes past, present, and future: you have the future in there all the time. So that's what I was trying to do, and if someone criticized me or attacked me or said something negative, it didn't really affect me because it didn't sound to me as if that was what I was. But I felt sorry for the people who hated me, for being so angry, because anger just hurts yourself."

"You once said, 'Hate is just an awkward way of love.' "

"That's right. And I was experimenting. For instance, when you see a person who's really angry, he's just completely concentrating on his anger, and you can sometimes even manage to make his emotions lighter."

"Do you mean that you focus on that anger and then transform that emotion for the person who's feeling it?"

"Yes."

"How do you do that?"

"I don't know, you just do it."

"You once asserted that 'he who has love and hatred has energy and will survive, but he who has no energy dies,' by which I took you to mean that love and hate are just different forms of energy. Because it's often been pointed out that the opposite of hate is actually indifference."

"That's true," she agreed. "Indifference is the most poisonous thing. You can definitely deal with hate but not with indifference."

"Nietzsche once suggested that we should all be courageous and *rebaptize* our negative emotions and be kind to them," I said, "sort of like turning lead into gold. And in a visionary text of yours called 'Rainbow Revelation,' which you wrote in 1985 after looking out the window and seeing a rainbow hovering like a mirage over Central Park, you proposed that we try to transform anger into versatility, greed into giving, jealousy into admiration, fear into flexibility, and sorrow into sympathy."

"Exactly."

"But you've also dealt with even more intense and painful emotions than those. In your song 'Approximately Infinite Universe,' you sing about a girl who's in constant hell because there are 'a thousand holes in her heart.' "

"Yes," Yoko said with a grim laugh, "that *was* me."

"And in the booklet for your album *Blueprint for a Sunrise*, you revealed something equally revelatory and painful when you wrote: 'Sometimes I wake up in the middle of the night hearing thousands of women screaming. Other times just one woman seems to try to talk to me.' There's also an artwork of yours called *Three Mounds* that consists of three piles of earth, and you explained that the first stands for women subjected to domestic violence, the second for women 'forced into madhouses,' and the third for women who are victims of elder abuse. Do you think that your personal pain has somehow enabled you to embrace other people's pain?"

"It's not so much my being *able* to do it, but it *happens*, and sometimes it's not very good for me—I often can't sleep at night. But I wish I had more healing powers, and I think that all of us should try to clean ourselves up because then our healing powers can more easily come out. And the reason why they don't come out, as I said to you before, is because we've been indoctrinated by religion to believe that we're not supposed to think about ourselves but about God, and so right away you're taking away everything that's good about *you* and not developing and letting that come forth. And in order to survive I try to keep on giving, giving. Just after John's passing, a lot of people were taking that opportunity to take a lot of his possessions, and it was a very difficult time for me. And I envisioned myself in the back of a truck, and the truck was moving, and all of these hyenas and wolves were running after it, and I just threw gold at them! That was just the comic side of it."

"For a profile I wrote about you in 1970, you talked a lot to me about how shy and fearful and anxious and lonely and scared you used to be, and about how you often felt like hiding and disappearing and becoming invisible. There's a novella written by the Japanese Nobel Prize winner Kenzaburo Oe called *Teach Us to Outgrow Our Madness.* How did you outgrow yours?"

"By bringing forth the pain I felt. And I was also aware that the power of communication allows you to connect with other forces that are actually *you.* I mean, the whole world is you."

"You once wrote a song called 'Angry Young Woman,' and in that song you advised the young woman to just keep walking and forget about her past, and assured her that 'when you turn the corner, you'll see the new world.' How did *you* go about turning the corner?"

"It just happened. It wasn't something contrived or intentional. Intentional is only half the game. If you turn the corner without contrived intention, you're in a world of magic in the sense that it's not just you but another thing that you meet—it might be the whole world, it might be the universe, it might be just one stone or pebble, but that's what makes the magic."

I reminded Yoko that when I had spoken to her in 1970 she told me about how she had gone to a palmist who informed her that she was like a very fast wind speeding around the world, but that she had just met a person who was fixed like a mountain and that he would be able to materialize her. But the palmist had also declared that John was himself *also* like a wind so that he was therefore able to understand her.

"Definitely," Yoko agreed. "But it's also true that I communicated with a mountain that is *me* as well."

"The mountain within you?"

"Yes. The mountain within me."

"I suspect that a lot of the more than three million people who follow you on Twitter and who are inspired by your message of peace and love aren't really aware of the painful things that you experienced when you were young, even before John's death."

"You know," Yoko told me, "when you look at the universe and the earth, there are so many people who didn't survive. The point is . . . Joan of Arc didn't survive. And I went through difficult things but I survived, and I feel very lucky. My wish is that *all* of us will heal together and use the incredible power each one of us has. I really have incredible hope for the human race."

Yoko's first and most famous book, *Grapefruit*, was published in 1964. Widely acknowledged as one of the most influential works of conceptual art, it has been in print for close to fifty years. Many of the book's readers, however, may not have noticed that almost every one of its instruction pieces and poems begins with a verbal imperative: Feel, Listen, See, Touch, Think, Find, Give, Stay, Remember, Imagine. After meditating on those words one day, it suddenly dawned on me that what all of them were ultimately instructing us to do was simply to *live*. And at that same moment I also realized that John Lennon's line "All we are saying is *give* peace a chance" revealed him to be one of Yoko's most accomplished students.

"*Live*." Yoko repeated the word to me. "Yes. Exactly. And it's all right to do that. We're all taught not to learn too much, not to think—all of the things you mentioned right now are often things that we're supposed *not* to do."

"Not to imagine, not to touch, not to feel."

"That's right."

"Maybe what you're ultimately saying is what the fifteenth-century Japanese Zen master Ikkyu once declared: 'Only one koan matters—*You!*' "

"And we've all lost ourselves," she said regretfully. "Isn't that sad? And I don't want to go away knowing that I've lost myself. And I also don't want anyone else to go away having lost themselves."

"A few years ago you gave me a special gift that I've always cherished—a bottle sealed with wax that contains within it a message written on a thin strip of paper. And that message consists of just one word, and the word is 'Remember.' I was wondering if you wouldn't mind my asking you whether you can recall your first memory."

"It's in a very strange way that I remember it," Yoko explained. "This is very strange—because my first memory was actually a recurring dream that I kept having when I was about two and a half or three years old. In the dream I was in the dark, like in a cave, and then a tiger appeared and roared, and when it roared, the darkness became even bigger and darker, and I was so scared. And then what happened was that I went through a very narrow tunnel, and at the end of the tunnel was a hospital room where I saw a table on which there was a surgical tray, and the room was lit with an unseen bare lightbulb. And I realized that that was how I was born."

"So your first memory was a dream of your being born?"

"Yes, isn't that amazing? And I was so scared. But I also had another kind of dream at that time—a happy dream—in which I was running around the house and laughing like crazy, and when I woke up I remember saying, please give me a dream like that one every night!"

One of Yoko's most haunting works is called *Vertical*

Memory, which consists of twenty-one photos and twenty-one accompanying texts. All the photos are identical and are a computerized amalgamation of the faces of Yoko's father, her husband, and her son. Each of the texts, however, is different, and each one briefly and dispassionately describes Yoko's encounters with various men—including her father as well as doctors, artists, and strangers—who had a profound effect on her life as it progresses, in *Vertical Memory*, from birth to death. The first text describes Doctor I, and it states: "I remember being born and looking into his eyes. He picked me up and slapped my bottom. I screamed." And the final and longest text describes an Attendant, and it begins: "I saw a dark hole in a shape of an arch. I saw my body being slid into it. It looked like the arch I came out of at birth, I thought. I asked where it was going to take me to. The guy stood there looking at me without saying a word." So I pointed out to Yoko that in her first "real" childhood memory, she is passing through a tunnel into life, but that in her last memory, as she describes it in *Vertical Memory*, she is passing through a tunnel into death.

"I know, it's so weird," Yoko said. "You go out and you go back in the same way. But don't forget that in *Vertical Memory* this was something that was artistically intended."

"It's also interesting," I added, "that in many patriarchal societies the female is legally beholden, first to her father, then to her husband, and finally to her son—all of whom are merged in your one photograph."

"Yes, you're their possession, and in *Vertical Memory* I wanted to symbolically express a woman's connection to men."

"Each one of the men you describe in your texts seemed to make you feel fearful and dependent. And at the conclusion of that last 'death text,' you write: 'It all seemed very familiar. What percentage of my life did I take it lying down? That was the last question I asked in my mind.' That statement really startled me, and I quoted it to a friend of mine and asked her your question: 'What percentage of your life did you take it lying down?' And my friend understood this question to refer to the sense of passivity."

"Yes," Yoko agreed, "passivity is what women have accepted in order to survive."

"With regard to the idea of remembrance, I wanted to relate to you an observation that an ancient Japanese emperor once made to his concubine. She had asked him what he thought the reasons and causes were that might explain our romantic involvements, and the emperor replied that because he believed that there was nothing sinful in the relationships between men and women since they were caused by bonds from former lives, they therefore defied our resistance. What do you think?"

"But I'm not sure all of this has to do with our bonds," Yoko responded. "It first starts off with our parents, and it's connected to that and we're stuck with that . . . and then it has to do with our other lives. But I don't believe that our bonds are the result just of the relationships we have in this society."

"Do you believe in reincarnation?"

"Yes. Off and on. But it's not just one life."

"Do you think that we choose our parents?"

"Half choose, maybe. Just like we half choose our actions every day, while the other half is something that just happens to you."

"There's that famous Japanese koan that goes: 'What did your face look like before your parents were born?' "

"But I'm not concentrating my mind on figuring out what that was," she responded. "It's more important that we respect and concentrate on our present life."

"Like everyone else," I said, "I know how important your bond with John was. And you've just published a beautiful color picture book called *An Invisible Flower* that touches on the mystery of that bond."

"It's something I did when I was a little girl," she told me, and then laughed. "Actually, I wrote and did the illustrations for the book in 1952 when I was nineteen years old."

"The book is about a flower that can't be seen but whose subtle odor travels over the sea and over the mountains and through the fields until, far away, a person named Smelty John smells it in the air . . . and then sneezes!"

"You know," she explained, "John did a drawing in 1952 when he was eleven years old in Liverpool that's on his *Walls and Bridges* album, and it shows a man and a woman, who look a little bit like John and me, riding on two horses, and on the drawing he signed it 'John W Lennon / To Mimi / 18th February 1952,' which was my nineteenth birthday!"

"It's always seemed to me," I said to her, "that there are three kinds of persons in the world: the one who says No, the one who says Maybe, and the one who says Yes. You once wrote a song called 'A Thousand Times Yes.' The word Yes appears on the ceiling of your famous *Ceiling Painting*. And I noticed that the last word of *An Invisible Flower* is also Yes. So even back when you were a teenager you were already a Yes person. Do you remember when it was that you first realized that you *were* a Yes person?"

"I think it was way back," Yoko replied. "My childhood wasn't easy. Everywhere I looked it was saying *no* to me. So I said yes, hoping that one day my life will be."

"One of my favorite lines from your songs occurs in 'You're the One': 'We were a wizard and a witch in a moment of freedom.' "

"You know," she told me, "I dedicated that song to John after his passing because when he was alive, he kept saying to me, 'I'm always writing love songs to you, but you never write love songs to me!' And the reason for that was because I was such a proud woman, and I didn't think that was important, especially when he had one hundred thousand fans."

"You mean one hundred million," I corrected her.

"Well, two hundred million, you know what I mean. So it wasn't a necessary song for me to write. But sometimes I felt that it was—'let me count the ways'—and especially when he passed away, that remark from John really came back to me. So I said, 'O.K., this is one I'm going to give to you,' and that was 'You're the One.' "

"John's song 'The Ballad of John and Yoko,' " I remarked, "contains what is for me one of the most consciousness-awakening things he ever wrote."

"What was that?"

"In that song he mentions that one night you told him that when you're dead, 'You don't take nothing with you / But your soul' . . . and, for a brief second in the song, John pauses and then shouts out the word: *'Think!'* And every time that I myself think about those lines, they remind me that I, too, should pause and figure out what I've been doing and how I've been living. Did you actually give him that advice?"

"Yes, I think so. And that's what I'm particularly doing these days because I don't really know how much time I have, and each day is so important. I feel like Mozart at the end of the film where he is just writing, writing, writing, making sure that he can finish it. I am doing that in all aspects of my life."

"In 'Mind Games,' " I said, "John encouraged all of us to keep 'pushing the barriers,' 'planting seeds,' and 'projecting our images in space and in time.' "

"And I think that's exactly what all of us are trying to do, but not well enough yet."

"It always seemed to me that in your and John's Bed-Ins for Peace, you were both trying to set a good example and were somehow suggesting in your own inimitable way that the entire world should try to become one gigantic Bed-In!"

"Yes," she said, laughing, "but also to relax and not to take it that seriously!"

"And in 'Imagine,'" I reminded her, "John proposed that we should all try to imagine sharing a peaceful world together and joining you and him to 'live as one.' There's an eighteenth-century Japanese poet named Issa who thought the same thing. He wrote: 'Under the cherry trees there are no strangers.'"

"That's like saying we should save the world with beauty," Yoko observed. "I love that line, and that's why I really think that art and creativity are so important—that tiny little poem by Issa is helping the world, changing the world, changing us. This is the first time I've encountered that poem, but it was always there, and it was affecting me even though I didn't know it.

"I recently read something—it was on an insert that I found in a weekend newspaper—and it said: 'Beauty will save the world.' You know what beauty is? It's something that you have to recognize in yourself, it's not something that you have to ask other people, 'Oh, is this supposed to be beautiful?' You should feel the beauty within. Actually, you don't have to feel the beauty within, but *within* you just feel the beauty of *everything.* You have to *feel* it. And that feeling is the world and all of us. We're all going to save the world together."

ACKNOWLEDGMENTS

Dear Sir or Madam will you read my book
It took me years to write, will you take a look?
—"PAPERBACK WRITER," THE BEATLES

For many years, I often thought that I would one day like to write a personal account of my relationship and friendship with John Lennon and Yoko Ono, whom I first met in London in September 1968. Forty-three years later—in 2011—I realized that it was now or never. And thanks to a number of extraordinary persons, I was given the opportunity to do so.

One afternoon over lunch, I explained to my literary agent, Steve Wasserman, that what I really wanted to do was to write a concise book from a solely personal perspective that would attempt to convey to the reader a sense of what it was like to have known and spent many memorable and spellbinding days and evenings with two of the most inspiring people I have ever met. So, as befitting such a book, Steve unusually suggested that, in lieu of a formal book proposal, I should simply write an informal letter to him saying exactly what I had told him, and that he would take it from there.

My "Dear Sir" letter fortunately found its way to Gerry Howard, the executive editor of Doubleday, who decided to chance it and edit the book himself. In their song "I Saw Her Standing There," the Beatles described how they suddenly stopped in their tracks upon catching sight on the dance floor of a seventeen-year-old girl who looked "way beyond compare." Little did I then know, but I was soon to discover, that I had been granted the opportunity to work with an editor who was himself "way beyond compare" and who had the uncommon ability to see hidden beneath the dross of a writer's first draft some inchoate intimations of literary redemption. Without Gerry's transformative editorial guidance it would not have been possible for me, for better or for worse, to complete *Days That I'll Remember.*

But my book would also not have been possible without the assistance of a number of other people.

At Doubleday, I am especially indebted to Hannah Wood, as well as to Bette Alexander, Karla Eoff, Joe Gallagher, Kristen Gastler, Lorraine Hyland, and Emily Mahon.

For their invaluable help, I am inestimably grateful to Jonas Herbsman and, at Studio One, to Andrew Kachel, Amanda Keeley, and Karla Merrifield.

For allowing me to use their remarkable photographs, I want to thank Ethan Russell, who took the photos that accompanied my first *Rolling Stone* interview with John Lennon in 1968, and Allan Tannenbaum.

For their abiding generosity and support, I give heartfelt thanks to Annie Druyan, Elizabeth Garnsey, Richard Gere, and Jann Wenner.

And I would also like to express my appreciation to Sonny Mehta for his having introduced me and my book project to Gerry Howard.

A French proverb says: "Gratitude is the heart's memory." And I am profoundly grateful to Yoko Ono for her enheartening encouragement and for the unstinting cooperation that she so generously provided me, while giving me carte blanche to write the book that I had dreamed of writing. As anyone who reads *Days That I'll Remember* will inescapably realize, I am, and have been for more than forty years, one of Yoko Ono's most devoted and unwavering fans. To me—as well as to innumerable people around the world—her life and work stand as an inspiring testimony to the powers of affirmation, imagination, compassion, and courage. John Lennon, of course, exemplified these same powers, and he sang about the "limitless undying love" that called him "on and on across the universe." It is fascinating to note that on January 12, 1983, the astronomer Brian A. Skiff at the Anderson Mesa Station of Arizona's Lowell Observatory discovered a minor planet, which he named *4147 Lennon*. John may have been only a minor planet, but he was a major star, shining on—just as he said we all do in his song "Instant Karma!"—like the moon and stars and the sun.

I will forever be thankful both to John Lennon and to Yoko Ono for having allowed me to share some indelible moments with them in the days of their lives.

ILLUSTRATION CREDITS